# Endorsements
## for Broken

Broken - Hands down- a FIVE star read for ALL leadership!! Dr. Murray's step-by-step process from a broken ministry to a triumphant life of grace is a must read for all ministers. Understanding Biblical restoration is vital for not only the broken, but the pastor or leader who is counseling the broken. As leader of the Assemblies of the Lord Jesus Christ, I have witnessed Dr. Murray's wise leadership on our general board and highly recommend his practical step-by-step guide to restoration.

**Rev. Kenneth Carpenter**
General Superintendent
Assemblies of the Lord Jesus Christ (ALJC)

"The Bible is full of Believers who have been "Broken" at one time or another. In like manner churches across the world are full with Believers who have been "Broken". Therefore the question that needs to be addressed is not that we as Believers make mistakes, but what do we do after the mistake is made? Well, your answer is right in your hands. In this powerful and life-changing book "Broken", my friend, Dr. Paul Murray will help you to get on the pathway of restoration. This book is rooted in Scripture, practical in it's game plan, and proven in the life of the author. Therefore I challenge each of you to find yourself a comfortable seat, open your heart, begin reading this book, and get RESTORED!!"

**Rev. Fred Luter, Past President**
Southern Baptist Convention (SBC)
Pastor - Franklin Avenue Baptist Church
New Orleans, LA

"Written with simplicity and honesty, Broken addresses failure in a practical and transparent manner as Dr. Murray intertwines his personal experience with powerful Biblical illustrations. This book is made complete with practical steps to guide one down their road to restoration."

**Bishop Lorenzo Hall, Presiding Prelate**
One Way Churches International (OWCI)
Pastor - Reach Out Apostolic Tabernacle
Martinsville, VA

"You'll never be the same! Dr. Paul Murray identifies with those who have failed. Broken is the state in which Dr. Murray presents his own history and personal failure and then builds a foundation for restoration through Scripture. I have known Dr. Murray for many years and have traveled the world with him. He has the heart of a servant, always concerned with helping his fellow man. An anointed prophet, his ministry has been a tremendous blessing at our national conventions, Pastoral leadership sessions, and in many of our churches throughout Brazil and the U.S.A. "Broken" illustrates how God is a God of second chances. It is written in a manner that magnifies God. And with the spirit of David, Dr. Murray, 'A man after God's own heart,' explains how you too can make it through. It's time to pick up the pieces of your broken life!"

**Bishop Dr. Manoel Ferreira**
President & General Superintendent
Brazilian Assemblies of God
Madureira Ministries
Brasilia, Brazil

"In a world where people habitually make excuses for sinful behavior, Dr. Murray is refreshingly candid as he weaves a tapestry of God's redemptive grace. In an hour when many believers are stymied by the pain of past failures, Broken exposes the cruel darkness of condemnation while at the same time embracing the light of Divine hope and forgiveness."

**Rev. Jay R. Stirnemann**
District Superintendent, Massachusetts-Rhode Island
United Pentecostal Church International (UPCI)
Pastor - Christ Temple United Pentecostal Church
Tiverton, RI

"No one can escape facing challenging moments in life where seemingly nothing makes any sense. Directions are blocked, visions are blurred, and all hope appears gone. I recommend reading Dr. Murray's brilliant, yet practical approach on how to regain your spiritual and psychological balance. "Broken" will assist you to affirm who you are and establish what you need to do to become WHOLE again--read "BROKEN"!!!

**Rev. Dr. Gerald L. Durley, Civil Rights Icon**
Pastor Emeritus - Providence Baptist Church
Atlanta, Georgia

"God has a plan for those who fail. If not, the failures of Biblical leaders such as David, Elijah and others would not grace the pages of Scripture. Dr. Paul Murray takes these, and other examples and shows the heart of God for redemption in the matters of everyday life, and sounds a note of hope for those "Broken" by thought, word and deed. In an age where so much of popular theology focuses on "success", Dr. Murray's book is a welcome balance to our prosperity culture."

**Dr. Howard Dean Trulear**
Director, Doctor of Ministry Program,
Howard University School of Divinity

"I would highly recommend this book to those who are dealing with failure and for the church as a whole. Broken illustrates the power of God's grace, the necessity of restoration, and the privilege to aide in such a process. The testimony comes after all the pieces are picked up!"

**Dr. Keith R. Anderson**
Student Health Records Office,
Director, Student Affairs Division
Practical Theology Department, Adjunct Professor
Liberty Baptist Theological Seminary
Senior Pastor - HiliFavrd Ministries,
Lynchburg VA

"This important book focuses on the most significant lesson along the journey to becoming both fully human & fully Christian: how to find restoration -- when failure inevitably meets us on the road. Out of the darkness of his own failure, Dr. Murray has written a personal testimony that has the bright ring of humble truth, a guidepost to all of us who, have like him, dwelt in the dark valley of failure. Drawing from his own life and rooted in Scripture, Broken offers us a deeply spiritual guidebook that will appeal to all those who seek to begin again after failure. Dr. Murray shows us not simply that it is possible -- but how to do it well. Bravo!"

**Rev. Mark Farr, President**
International Institute for Sustained Dialogue
Washington, DC

# BROKEN

Picking up the Pieces After the Fall

*"The ultimate measure of a man is not where he stands in moments of comfort, but where he stands at times of challenge and controversy."*
– **Rev. Dr. Martin Luther King, Jr.**

*Foreword by New York Times Best Seller*
## Dr. Robert A. Schuller

# BROKEN
## Picking Up the Pieces After the Fall

## Dr. Paul Murray

# Copyright

©Broken: Picking up the pieces after the fall.
by Dr. Paul Murray 2012
Edited by Grant Rahme
Book Servicing by B.O.S.S. Publishing ~~ www.boss-publishing.com
Cover Designed by Emmanuel Johnson
Interior Designed by Howard Clay

All rights reserved. Under International Copyright Law, no part of this publication may be reproduced, stored, or transmitted by any means- electronic, mechanical, photographic (photocopy), recorded, or otherwise- without written permission.
For information address B.O.S.S. Publishing at
P.O.Box 371612
Decatur, GA 30037

For information regarding special discounts for bulk purchases, sales promotions, speaking engagements and or book clubs. For details, please contact
B.O.S.S. Publishing
Email: Contact@boss-publishing.com

Manufactured in the United States of America

ISBN: 978-0-9863559-1-2 (Hard Cover)
ISBN: 978-0-9863559-2-9 (Soft Cover)
Library of Congress Number: 2015905107

Because of the dynamic nature of the Internet, any web addresses or links contained in this book may have changed since publication and may no longer be valid.

10 9 8 7 6 5 4 3 2

# Content

| | |
|---|---|
| Dedication | I |
| Acknowledgements | II |
| Foreword by: | |
| Dr. Robert A. Schuller | VI |
| Rev. Robert W. Martin | X |
| Introduction | 1 |
| **Chapter One:** | |
| Failure Is Not Final | 5 |
| **Chapter Two:** | |
| What We Do In Secret Are Seeds Planted in Our Souls | 20 |
| **Chapter Three:** | |
| Turning Regrets into Positive Action | 26 |
| **Chapter Four:** | |
| Moving Past Your Failure – How God's Servants Did It | 34 |
| **Chapter Five:** | |
| The Wisdom To Deal with Failure | 46 |
| **Chapter Six:** | |
| Finding God When Others Have Abandoned You | 58 |
| **Chapter Seven:** | |
| Finding Forgiveness Starts With You | 70 |
| **Chapter Eight:** | |
| Rejection is God's Protection | 86 |
| **Chapter Nine:** | |
| Rebuilding Your Credibility | 98 |
| **Chapter Ten:** | |
| Picking Up The Pieces | 112 |
| **Chapter Eleven:** | |
| Focus on Your Everyday Successes | 122 |
| **Chapter Twelve:** | |
| The Restoration Of A Failure – A Biblical Perspective | 134 |
| **Chapter Thirteen:** | |
| The Role of Leadership in Restoration | 148 |
| **Chapter Fourteen:** | |
| Personal Transformation | 168 |
| **Chapter Fifteen:** | |
| Understand Why God Allowed you to Experience Failure | 182 |
| **Chapter Sixteen:** | |
| Understanding How Sharing Your Failure Fits God's Plan For Your Life | 198 |
| Conclusion: | |
| In All Things God Works For The Good Of Those Who Love Him | 206 |
| **Endnotes:** | 220 |
| **About the Author** | 236 |

## This book is dedicated to

My Lord and Savior Jesus Christ, a merciful and loving God who took me out of the muck and mire of my sinful state and planted my feet on a solid rock.

To my wonderful children, Tamryne, Mekaila and, Caleb. There is one thing I desire for each of you to grasp in your life's journey, and that is, when you fall…. You can get back up.

And to my precious wife, Rachel, you are God's greatest gift to me. A godly woman with unconditional love who has never left my side – through all of life's ups and downs, you remain my prayer warrior, my protector, my best friend, and the love of my life.

II

# Acknowledgements

What follows is motivated by my passionate desire to help others in a spiritual and practical manner. I desire to demonstrate through my own testimonies and through the solid truth of God's Holy Word that no matter how low you have fallen or how great the failure, hope is still available. I have learned that even though failure is not forgotten, it certainly is not final.

It has been no easy task to present myself to you, the public, with such vivid transparency and vulnerability as I transcribe my thoughts and pains, my ups and downs, into a book that reveals the brokenness and failures of my own life. Yet this is perhaps the best manner in which I am able to provide a pathway to restoration for others. This journey would not be what it is without the mercy and grace of my Lord and Savior. If He did not whisper into my ears seeds of hope in the darkest days of my life, and direct me through His transformative words, I know I would not be here today.

I sometimes consider the Old Testament story of Job, who was a righteous man. Because of his integrity and faithfulness he was attacked, and through his time of suffering, his friends became unsupportive and kept their distance. His wife even called on him to curse God and die. In light of Job's story, I then consider my past and my own failure, and this brings me to the realization of how truly blessed I am, and in comparison to Job, how undeserving I am of such grace. I am blessed because my God is greater than my enemies, more compassionate than my naysayers, and continuously extends His mercy and grace.

A big thanks to all those from B.O.S.S. Publishers who have worked so hard and helped in making my dream become a reality. From the photo shoots to the social media campaign and all the meetings in between, it has truly been a great experience. And to my incredible editor, Grant Rahme and the input from his brother Hilton. Grant worked tirelessly as he guided me through my first experience in writing a book to make sure that this finished product was excellent.

I want to thank my church members who loved me, stood by me, and aided me. And special thanks to Elder, Jim Sears, and his wife, Margaret; Bobby and Sherry Simpson; Eddie and Lillian Sears; and William Denton. They have been with me throughout my brokenness and restoration and are still doing the work of His Kingdom by my side.

A deep appreciation, respect, and thank you to Mr. Jim Flynn, International President of the Global Peace Foundation, for allowing me to be a part of something great, working with me, and being a friend. You truly are the embodiment of a moral and innovative leader.

I am so blessed because God has provided me with some genuine friendships. Thanks to those dear friends who remained true and had no problem with calling me friend. To Rev. Tracy and Amy Zimmerman, your many years of friendship and support hold more value than all the treasures on earth. To Rev. Rodney Dame, I am so proud of what God has done and continues to do in your life. I am honored to call you friend, but honored so much more that you call me friend. And to Rev. John & Djuana Smith III, your many words of encouragement, ministry, genuine friendship, and all those times of fellowship kept my head above water and my heart focused on Jesus. Because of each of you, I have been the recipient of God's mercy and grace through your love and unfailing support.

To my father-in-law and mother-in-law, Bishop Douglas and Caroline Chesson, you both clearly let me know I am family. You demonstrated in actions your real love for me and put everything on the line to stand with me and by me. You are not only family to me, but my mentors and closest of confidants.

And through these many years, to my mother and brothers, thank you for your love. In memory of my father who I am proud to have called my Dad and who I truly miss. I am so thankful for all the times we had together and just knowing how much you loved me fills the void of your presence until we meet again in heaven. And with a profound love for my identical twin brother, Phillip, who throughout our life has had to deal with the repercussions of my actions just because we looked alike! I am so grateful for your love and our bond that continues to deepen and grow stronger every day – you are my brother by birth, but we are best friends by choice. To my many new friends who I've shared my story with, you have made the road to restoration refreshing and achievable. I thank you for your willingness to not allow my past to define me and for believing in who I am now and what God continues to do in and through me.

And as I recognized in the dedication portion of this book, I would like to acknowledge God, my children, and my wife – I cannot be a more blessed man in all the world or throughout all of history. And especially to my precious wife, Rachel, who unabashedly and steadfastly remains by my side. You have picked me up when I was down, shielded me when I was vulnerable, and loved me with all that is within you. I have seen in you how God's Word – which speaks of being my rock and my fortress – has been manifested in and through you! Thank you. I love you with all my heart.

# Foreword

## Dr. Robert Schuller
*New York Times Best Seller*

Have you ever felt like you want to hit the restart button of your life? Have you ever done something that you are ashamed of and will do anything to keep it covered up? Have or do you feel like you are living a lie and pray that it will never come to light? If your life were an open book, who would be hurt, which morals would be stretched or what broken laws would be revealed?

Operating in the shadows of secrets is a debilitating, life strangling, and joy squelching way to exist. This is not the way God wants you or me or anyone to live. God wants us to live in the light of truth, to experience the grace of his forgiveness, and to drink from his cup so that we will never thirst again. He wants us to enjoy an abundant life.

This will only happen when we become cleansed from our past mistakes and step out of the shadows and into the light. In order for us to be able to do this there are certain steps we need to take. It is not easy. It is painful. There are prices to be paid and changes to be made but in the end it is worth every penny and every tear that it costs. Living in darkness leads to death. Living in the light leads to life. Dr. Paul Murray will show you the secrets of how to leave the dark life and enter the marvelous light of Christ.

Dr. Paul Murray and I have been friends for many years. I met him through the Global Peace Foundation in 2008 in Brasília, Brazil. While attending the GPF conference I met many people who I have grown to love and admire over the years. Paul is at the top of that list. His open and honest spirit is heart warming and endearing. I have watched him raise a family, grind his way through a doctoral program at Howard University, pastor a church, lead and grow the Coalition for American Renewal, travel around the world for international peace, and now, he has written this book.

The miracle of Broken is evident in the way the Holy Spirit has guided Dr. Murray to write in a manner that draws the shattered lives of the fallen into the mighty presence of God. This book explains why I love and admire Paul so much. It explains how he can be so down to earth, real and approachable. He openly shares his failed past and how he got through those deep lonely dark valleys. He explains his own journey and uses it as a map for you.

Nothing is lost throughout these pages: From the call to repentance to the need for accountability; from the promised blessings of God to the gift of a restored life in Christ. As you continue your life path, allow the words that Dr. Murray shares to guide you and light up your life. You will be glad you did. It will make all the difference in the world.

Step out in faith today. The first step is easy. Read the book. The second step will be much more difficult, but not impossible. Just remember always that God loves you just the way you are with all your flaws and failures. He brought you to this book because He wants to help you help yourself. It begins today. It begins now.

FOREWORD: Dr. Robert Schuller

x

# Foreword

## Rev. Robert W. Martin

Former General Superintendent
Assemblies of the Lord Jesus Christ (ALJC)
Pastor - Voice of Pentecost
Baton Rouge, Louisiana

"Isaiah said of the Lord that "a bruised reed he will not break." Sadly, God's persuasion is not always the same as man's. For a multitude of reasons, restoration is not always the preferred action of people, although it is a sign of the truly spiritual, according to Paul in Galatians ("Brethren, if a man be overtaken in a fault, ye which are spiritual, restore such an one . . ."). Contrary to what I have heard ministers espouse through the years, people are not replaceable. Someone else cannot do what you can do because your sphere of influence is uniquely yours. Therefore the need for and God's desire to restore. Truly, God does not want to replace people; He wants to restore them.

Dr. Murray presents to us an incredible book on an extremely important topic. With rare transparency and candor, he skillfully uses the Bible to reveal God's heart to restore and why it is necessary. Dr. Murray also provides practical steps to help the fallen to be restored. He provides needed guidelines to help the broken pick up the pieces and to use their points of brokenness as strengths, for themselves and for others.

Dr. Murray's tale is very personal and inspiring. His "fall" did not precipitate his demise, but rather it helped to form him into the important and influential voice he is in the Christian community today.

We have all fallen. We have all been broken. Some are more public than others, but regardless it is a common human experience. May we as the 21st century church depart from our oft-engrained Pharisaical ways and reach a hand down to each other. Otherwise, sadly, the church dies one broken person at a time. Thank you Dr. Murray for convicting me, helping me, and encouraging me to seek the true heart of God for restoration. Read this book and apply its precepts. Don't break what God refuses to break. Become a Christian in action as well as in word".

FOREWORD: Rev. Robert W. Martin

# Introduction

*"This is a faithful saying, and worthy of all acceptation, that Christ Jesus came into this world to save sinners; of whom I am chief."*
**– I Timothy 1:15[1](KJV)**

I just could not understand it. The pastors and ministers I knew well, prayed with, fellowshipped with, even cried with, and helped in their times of need... These were the pastors and leaders I had served under and served with all my heart, still willing to be of service, and doing all I could to be their friend. I thought for sure if there was any group of people who would show mercy, that would help me, for sure it would be them... my friends, my mentors, these wonderful men and women of God.

I was staring at the greatest failure in my life as it was made public. I was not looking for anyone to push it under the rug and act like it never happened. No! I knew I had failed and I wanted to take responsibility for it. I wanted to stand up and make it right. But I was afraid. In my desire to look good, I had taken shortcuts, operated in the "gray" areas

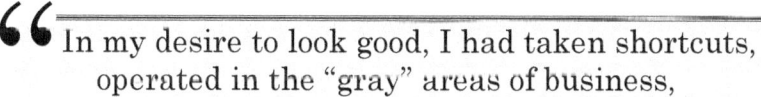
> In my desire to look good, I had taken shortcuts, operated in the "gray" areas of business,

of business, and done what I could to justify my actions. My justification was based on what I had seen others doing, and so I chalked up my actions to: "this is just how business is done." I based all my actions on wanting to maintain a public image of success. In other words, it was my pride that drove me over the edge into failure.

That public image of success which I worked hard to maintain was transformed overnight into a public image of disgrace! I crossed a line that could not be moved. I sold my integrity, my moral values, and my character – for what? A few accolades? The praise of people? I should have known better! All the good I had done: the awards; the accomplishments; my standing in the community... these all evaporated the moment my transgression became public.

In my fear, uncertainty and shame, I sought for mercy and refuge from the public gossip and ridicule, and so I turned to the men and women of God I knew. Yet, I was mortified that in turning to those leaders and ministers within my church organization, I instead received greater condemnation, and even attacks on my ministry. I was shunned, pushed away and treated as an outcast, like a leper diseased for the rest of my natural life. During this experience, I remembered what my twin brother said to me once – "I've been treated better by people in the world, than by people in the church." I was now living the very embodiment of that statement – I would often think, "Nothing like kicking a man when he is down"!

I knew in my heart and mind I was not running to them so they could give me a little slap on the hand and a message that said, "Oh, don't worry, we'll just forget about it." I hoped for a place I could go to for spiritual guidance and emotional support. I clearly understood that things would not be the same as a result of my own failure. But I needed a place where I could go to, bruised and battered, and yet, regardless of my fault, still be forgiven and guided by the elders of God's church, while walking down

> But I needed a place where I could go to, bruised and battered..

that long road to restoration. Well, it didn't happen that way.

As you are reading this book, you have probably guessed that I "made it!" I made it through this life-altering experience years ago only by the grace of God and the love and support of a few good people: my precious wife, a true woman of God; my wife's parents, who stood by me and loved me unconditionally; and a few very close friends who remained friends. After all these years, I look back and I am not bitter towards my pastors, mentors and friends. In my own imperfections, I learned that I can never stand in judgment against another, but rather, I must always extend a hand of mercy and be a friend – for that is what God gave to me.

You do not have to be famous to have your dirty laundry aired in public! Whether or not you believe in God, whether you attend a church

> You do not have to be famous to have your dirty laundry aired in public!

or have attended a church at some time, and you have failed publicly in some area, remember this basic truth: sin is no respecter of persons. The Bible is very clear on the subject: "For all have sinned, and come short of the glory of God."[3]

If you are not sure about God and even wonder why you picked up this book or why it was given to you, it is for this precise reason that God has placed my testimony into your hands. God wants to personally demonstrate to you that He is real and He loves you. In fact, God wants all human beings to hold onto this promise: He will never leave you nor forsake you. The journey for you begins by believing in Him.

Let me remind you that sin is sin. Whether you broke the law of the land or God's law, it separates you from Him; destroys relationships; shuts the door on future opportunities, and puts your life as you once knew it on hold indefinitely. You are no longer recognized for who you are, but rather for what you have done.

To move from private or public failure to a renewed life, restored relationships, and positive standing will not happen automatically. It will only happen when you allow God into the equation and then do what is required from your side to rectify the situation. There will still be days of doubt, depression, and even those times of wishing to just end it all! I have experienced all of these emotions and more, many more times than I care to remember. However, for me, underneath all of these negative thoughts there was a still, small voice that kept me moving even when my feet didn't want to. Kept me looking ahead even when everything within me was trying to look back. Kept me protected even when I was emotionally naked, ashamed, and vulnerable. The revelation of overcoming was revealed to me only after I had overcome – initially, all I heard were the whispers of God's voice speaking into my heart and telling me that He was giving me another chance. He was guiding me as I began to pick up the pieces of my broken life. Through this process, God demonstrated His love for me by giving me another chance, just like He had done so many times before. In other words, He wasn't done with me yet.

He is telling you right now, He is not done with you either! Irrespective of your current relationship with Him, your station in life or what you have done wrong, I pray right now that as you read this book, the Holy Spirit will comfort you, challenge you, and guide you. I have written in a manner that expounds upon His Word. Using my personal life experiences, I have set out to impart the necessary requirements for you to follow as laid out by God in His Word, which will enable you to travel down that road to restoration. I want you to truly experience the God of a second chance, as He seeks to take your brokenness and transform you. If you allow God to help you, you will already have taken the first step in picking up the pieces of your life that were shattered as a result of your failure.

> " I want you to truly experience the God of a second chance...

# Chapter One
## Failure Is Not Final[4]

*"For a just man falleth seven times, and riseth up again: but the wicked shall fall into mischief."*
**– Proverbs 24:16**[7]

Failure hurts! It's disappointing, embarrassing and humiliating. There is a measure of shame that is associated with failure. For some, the weight of shame they will carry is dependent upon how "public" their failure has been. Essentially, shame is a

> " ...shame is a subcategory of fear, and fear is what keeps you isolated...

subcategory of fear, and fear is what keeps you isolated, keeps your head hanging low, and is what drives your inability to make eye contact with others. With fear as your bedmate, you hide from the world and from God because you have put on a covering of shame.

In the Garden of Eden, after Adam sinned, when God began to speak to him, he covered himself behind brush before God as a testament of his own shame. I have read and even been told by some that there are benefits to failure. I know from personal experience that when failure is handled appropriately it can build character, teach compassion and make one humble.

I know firsthand how true these statements are, yet it cannot take away from the fact that failure still hurts! It hurts the one who failed and those around that person. When a person fails, it can be likened to a rock thrown into the middle of a pond. As that individual plunges in their failure, there is a ripple effect which takes place on the surface of the pond. The side effects quickly and quietly move through the lives surrounding the one who has failed. The inner circle – spouse, children, parents – all feel the wave of shock, hurt, humiliation, and even anger roll over them. These feelings move outward to friends and associates, neighbors and coworkers. Failure moves proportionately through your

 *Failure moves proportionately through your circle of influences. No one is untouched…*

circle of influences. No one is untouched, and this is why failure can be so devastating. Like a rock thrown into the pond, there is a feeling that all is over and there will never be another chance to be picked up from the depths of your sin and misery to be placed once again on dry land.

The preeminent reason for writing this book for each of you who have failed, messed up, or more pointedly, sinned against God, is to reaffirm God's holy and immutable words of promise and hope for you and your loved ones. I write also to reassure you of your future in Christ Jesus. As a leader, I write to other leaders to stress the importance of following God's Biblical mandates in guiding those who have failed. As leaders, we have a moral obligation to assist those in our care by setting them on the path to restoration. In addressing failure, I have focused upon those failures in life that are a direct result of sin. Some may say my words are just an attempt to sugar-coat sin by calling it "failure." This is far from my actual intention and opposes the message God has placed in my heart. In essence, when we have sinned, we have failed God, along with those who our sin has had an impact upon. As you sit there and wonder how you will be able to put your life back together, do not be dismayed.

As you read this book, my prayer for you is that God will impart to you the promised hope which is found in the measure of faith He has given to you. You can at this very moment begin to move from a setback in your life towards a setup for God, so He can do something great in you and through you.

God, in His Word and through His demonstration of love for each of us, robed Himself in flesh and died on Calvary's cross to secure the promise of hope and forgiveness for all who seek Him. How you handle your failure will determine whether you move forward and live a more abundant life through the humbling experience of failure or whether you will be defeated by your inaction, self-pity, denial and lack of accountability. If you choose to move forward rather than to accept defeat, drawing in faith from the Words and Spirit of Christ Jesus will be the power driving your motion.

As demonstrated in my introduction, I am not writing as one who sits above another in judgment or one that considers himself better than anyone else; far from it. As your narrator, I speak from my own personal experiences and knowledge. I cannot take you on a journey

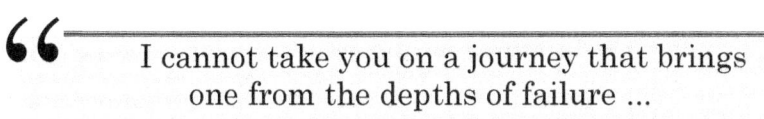

> I cannot take you on a journey that brings one from the depths of failure ...

that brings one from the depths of failure to the heights of God's grace and restoration if I had not been there myself.

My failure is not unique, in that my journey is the result of taking many small steps in the wrong direction. It is unique in that it is my story, my struggle, my awakening, and my journey from a broken vessel to one restored. For me, the fall came after leaving an organization I was leading that was preparing to close its doors. As it's director, I could not bring in the revenue to keep it up and running. I handed in my resignation and took up another position only to receive a phone call months later, filled with many difficult questions.

The questions related to money that was awarded to the organization through a grant. I was asked why this money was used for operational expenses rather than the designated building project for which it had been allocated. Because the funds were misappropriated, the funder wanted the money back. This put the organization in a difficult situation. It also raised questions about me as facilitator of the budget, and my handling of the operation. This misappropriation of funds opened a Pandora's box on my many 'gray' areas of administrative management. In my own mind, however, I was simply following the typical routine of borrowing from Peter to pay Paul, which is something I assumed everyone in the non-profit sector did. I had the good intention of raising the revenue to complete the funded project, yet this intention never materialized. In other words, I came to the realization and revelation that I had broken the law. My standard for business ethics had been operating in the red, and as a result, everything I had done was scrutinized under a microscope.

As I reflect on this failure, I remember that I compartmentalized the way I did business and the way I did ministry. I held myself to a very high standard in ministry, and would never have managed my administrative responsibilities in such a loose fashion, nor operated in such a questionable manner. I understood both the responsibility and accountability I had to God in ministry, knowing what I did could affect for eternity the lives of those to whom I ministered. Unfortunately, I did not reflect the same ethics in my role as director of an organization. In my effort to look good and maintain a status of success, I left my morals and

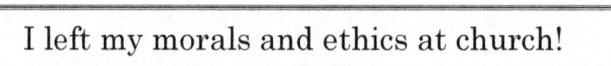

> I left my morals and ethics at church!

ethics at church! Overnight, I found my life unraveling, as my operational management revealed unethical behavior and even an illegal act that, at the time, I did not even realize I had perpetrated. Using designated funds for something else is illegal, no matter what my intentions were at the time. Regardless of the fact that I had informed board members about how the money was being used, I had still broken the law and would be held accountable.

It felt as if I had been hit in the face with a brick. Things went from bad to worse when several other actions – also unethical in nature – came to light and did even further damage. I failed and did so miserably. My failure was a direct result of my sinful actions. I could not claim ignorance, nor could I blame my decisions on the board. It was all the little things I did which added up to bring about my downfall. Therefore, when it comes to failure and sin, I have been an unwilling – and shamefully at times like this – a willing participant. Failure does not happen all at once. For those

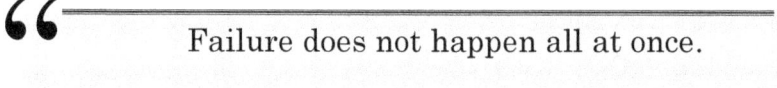

of you who have failed, as you take time to reflect on your own situation while reading this book, you will notice your failure was gradual, much like my own. It happened little by little over time as you allowed one small decision after another to slip by, in spite of knowing it wasn't right.

It reminds me of the cartoon of a snowball going down a hill. It starts off small and slow but as it goes down the hill, the snowball grows and picks up momentum. Our human lives have a similar way of gathering momentum. Before you know it, those seemingly insignificant lies, minor indiscretions, and grasped opportunities to cheat have accumulated over time. You suddenly find that the momentum of your accumulated transgressions has picked up and you are unable to prevent yourself from hurtling down a hill at breakneck speed. And in that moment, a shock of realization hits you – you have lost control! You wake up to find yourself smashed against a fence at the bottom of the hill! My sin stripped away the sanctity of my salvation and separated me from the presence of God. But, I thank God for His mercy, His forgiveness, His blood covering, and His long-suffering toward me. It was His death on Calvary's cross that redeemed my ticket to hell for a mansion in heaven.

I learned from my own harsh experience that repentance is the key to escaping from the pit we sometimes find ourselves in. Just saying you

 The most critical step in rising up out of a pit of failure is to acknowledge your own actions…

are sorry is not repentance. Blaming the actions of others for your own demise does not cut it either. The most critical step in rising up out of a pit of failure is to acknowledge your own actions – the actions that brought you to where you are. Without taking this first, open, honest and self-examinational step, you will never be able to move forward.

The day I received that interrogatory call, I knew I had to be honest about my actions. Questions were asked about what I did and did not do; how I spent the revenues raised; the authenticity of the reports I created, and so on. I knew exactly what I had done wrong and also what I had done correctly. I understood that the situation could become a whole lot worse if I did not speak the truth. At that moment I thought of my standing in the community, my role as a pastor, and my responsibility as a husband and father. Everything was up in the air and uncertain. The first thing I did was to start praying to God, asking Him to forgive me for my sins. Next, I asked God for His guidance. Then I spoke to my wife. We cried, discussed the situation, and said another prayer together. She took my hand, and as she hugged me, I knew that if I lost everything else, at least I would still have her. In her wisdom and understanding of my confession, she was not naïve to the gravity of my situation, nor did she consider my confession to be unnecessary. We both knew I had failed, and as a result, I had disappointed many people. What I now needed to do was to examine my actions with complete honesty in order to identify exactly where I had gone wrong and begin to make things right.

This self-examination did not happen in one sitting but took time, as I answered questions, reviewed information and reflected on what I had done. Some of the questions raised reminded me of certain slipshod actions I had taken, while other things, which I had thought were within

## Chapter One: Failure Is Not Final

the scope of my authority, turned out not to be. In addition to the use of designated funds being transferred into the account that kept our operations in motion, there were three other notable actions I was guilty of that were unethical and even dishonest in nature. Holding the position of director, I was very fortunate to have had several good people working for me. One particular individual was strapped financially, so once a month when we did our shopping for the business, I would tell her to buy what she needed. I told her she was a valued employee and although I could not pay her in cash for the value she was worth, I could at least compensate her in this fashion. This was not a one-time incident either – I did this every time we went shopping. I did not have board of directors approval for such an action, and even though I did not personally benefit, I did not have the authority to make this decision. As a result, I was held personally responsible for these expenditures.

The second notable action I was guilty of is something I did not consider to be an issue, but quickly found out to the contrary. One of those crazy things many of us don't do when we are issued a new credit card is to read the fine print. I ordered a credit card for the business and used it when necessary. I was also using it for personal items, never giving this a second thought. The problem, I soon found out, was that because it was a corporate card, it could not be used for personal purchases. When the monthly bill came in, I would write a check out of my personal account to cover my expenses, while using business funds to pay for business expenditures. As it turned out, when I was under investigation and all these credit card charges were identified, it was assumed that the business had paid for all my personal expenses too. Although this

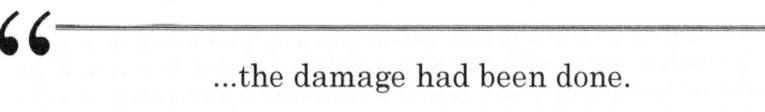

> ...the damage had been done.

was not the case, and I promptly produced all my canceled checks to verify this fact, the damage had been done. Within the broader scope of everything else that had taken place, this really did not matter too much. Yet the fact remains that I was wrong and did not have permission to use the card in such a manner.

As our operations were sinking deeper into a financial hole, I stepped over the gray area and sunk the final nail into my own coffin. At the end of each month, I would present a report to the board, informing them about what funds and donations were coming in. Because I wanted the board to think I was bringing in big revenue, I hatched a devious plan. I thought it would be smart to open up a separate checking account in the business name and then deposit all the small checks into that account. At the end of the month I would write one large check from the new account and deposit it into the main business account to reflect this seemingly large contribution I had been able to obtain. I knew flat out when I was doing this, that it was wrong. However, by this time, all my little white lies and fudging caught up to me. I justified this action by believing that if I had a little more time, I could turn things around, but – as is almost always the case when one thinks his or her actions justify the end – it never happened. I had no answer, but yes, I did that and I am sorry. By not giving my vocation the same standard and integrity I gave my ministry, I failed everyone associated with me in every sphere of my life – business, ministry, community, friends, and family.

Let me remind you, when you have sinned, you have failed God. It does not matter what your title may be, your position, how much money you have, nor does it matter how many years you have served the Lord. Even a child of God is not immune to failure. And let me add to this that

> " Even a child of God is not immune to failure.

it does not matter whether your failure is public or private. Of these two, the private failures are the most dangerous. Private failure will build upon itself, and when it does eventually become public – and it will – it will have an even greater power to completely destroy you.

If your failure is from immoral, illegal, or unethical actions or even a combination of these, they automatically strip away your veneer and mark you as an outcast. This is all caused by the accumulation of sinful actions that now result in a public or private revelation of failure. I personally have felt the pain of failure as it ripped away what little layer of integrity and character that was used as my covering. I am well aware that the Bible tells us, "all have sinned, and come short of the glory of God."[5] Yet, this is not a license or excuse for sin, but rather a battle in which we are engaged, and which we need to understand, between our fleshly desires, our human mind, and our spirit.

Failure affects three specific categories of people: those addressing others who fail (I am referring to those in leadership within ministry); those who are close to or connected in some way to the one who failed; and the one who has failed. Let me address each group separately as a precursor to the instructions and guidance that will be offered in the coming chapters.

**FOR THOSE IN MINISTRY ADDRESSING OTHERS WHO FAIL:**

When addressing the failure of others, love and kindness must be your calling card. No servant of God has the authority to take a broken and battered vessel and be so quick to throw it in the fire, for God has

> When addressing the failure of others, love and kindness must be your calling card.

placed a great value on that very soul. We cannot be judgmental against one who has failed, but neither can we excuse it. The most important duty that each of us have as God's servants is to assist in the restoration of any willing vessel. Chapter thirteen speaks directly to you and your approach.

**FOR THOSE CLOSE TO THE ONE WHO HAS FAILED:**

As you struggle with the hurt and embarrassment caused by a loved one, friend or member of the body of Christ, remember that God is calling you to be the vessel His Holy Spirit can move through. A vessel that has within it all that is necessary to serve as an anchor for that fallen loved one or friend.

For every minister, friend, and loved one attempting to discern the actions and reasons for another person's failure, please understand –

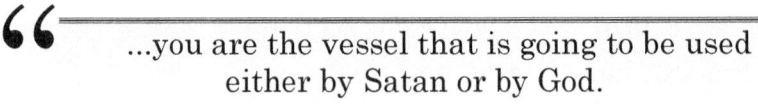

> ...you are the vessel that is going to be used either by Satan or by God.

you are the vessel that is going to be used either by Satan or by God. Your actions, inactions and reactions will be a true testament to what you believe, and whether you will use what you have received from God concerning mercy, forgiveness, compassion and most importantly, love... or whether you stand in a place of judgment and public condemnation. I pray these pages will fill you with God's compassion for the broken and backslidden. So much so, that when you put this book down, you will clothe yourself with the garments of a Samaritan and truly serve those who need you most.

**FOR YOU WHO ARE DEALING WITH FAILURE:**

You are currently facing a failure in your life and may feel there is no hope in tomorrow. Your first step is to be honest with yourself. It is so easy to point a finger at all those who helped trip you up, those who have come against you wrongfully after the failure has become public, and those who said they would be there, only to turn against you. Like Adam, we can blame the "Eve's" in our lives, but we are all responsible for our own actions. If you can grasp this one point, it will revolutionize your whole perspective and will be the vehicle that moves you from the agony of failure to a restorative and glorious work through Christ. You have the opportunity and ability through Jesus to transform the present and past failures in your life into a victorious testimony of the mercy and restoring power of our Lord and Savior, Jesus Christ.

Hang onto this promise – God will see you through! When the naysayers and bystanders take hold of your sin and shout out for all to hear that they will forgive you, but your failure will never be forgotten, know that God does not operate in such a manner. As a minister of the Gospel who has failed, I know all too well the contradictions exemplified in our peers and even well intentioned people of God. The Bible tells us to forgive, to restore one who falls (fails) among you – yet too often, we see the cursory move of the lips as the words are formed. We hear the words of forgiveness as they are spoken, but while these words quickly dissipate, the actions necessary to bring life to such words never materialize.

I have learned through these experiences how true it is to keep your eyes on the Lord and not humankind. People will fail you! Friends will fail you, family will fail you, even ministers and pastors will fail you. Now,

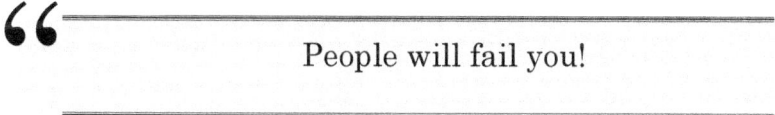

People will fail you!

as you quickly agree to this statement, pause for a moment to consider: "What makes them any different than you?" They fail you and me because they are human just like you and me! We all are born into sin and shapen into iniquity.[6] It doesn't matter how many degrees hang on their walls, or who they are connected to, or even how many years they have served in ministry. They deal with and have dealt with failures in their own lives too. Now, that should make you feel a little better, but it is not a "get out of jail card." Their actions, inactions, and inappropriate reactions cannot and will not justify your own.

Herein lies the primary ingredient to every testimony of failure that has been transformed into success by the loving hand and mercy of Jesus Christ: do not focus on who has failed you, but focus on your own failure

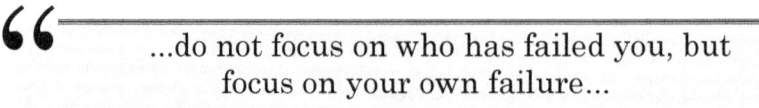

and what you are going to do about it! It can only start with you. It's that simple – yet that powerful. You are in control of your own destiny. Do you turn it over to Satan... to your flesh, or are you willing to humble yourself before God and let Him begin a new work in you?

**FAILURE IS NOT FINAL... UNLESS YOU ALLOW IT TO BE.**

If you are like most people, when you fail, you are inundated with doubts about your intelligence, your abilities and your worth. You are embarrassed and tempted to give up. Don't! At least not until you've considered God's record for transforming failures, for turning life's misfits and rejects into dynamic men and women of worth.

Think about the following men and women of God that are forever mentioned in His holy Word, and how God used them to save nations, protect generations, and used His anointing for the deliverance of many. Take a look at the Scriptures and you will find that Noah was a drunk, Jacob was a liar, Joseph was abused, Moses was a murderer, Samson was a womanizer, Rahab was a prostitute, David was an adulterer and a murderer, Elijah was suicidal, Jonah ran from God, Peter denied Jesus, the disciples fell a sleep while praying, and Martha worried about everything!

*"The just man falls, sometimes falls seven times perhaps, into sin, sins of infirmity through the surprise of temptation; but he rises again by*

*repentance, finds mercy with God, and regains his peace." (Matthew Henry Commentary on Proverbs 24:16)*[7]

What am I trying to say? Just this: failure isn't final. Secular history also has its successful failures, the two most notable being Abraham Lincoln and Winston Churchill. Both men rose to power in an hour of crisis in their nation's history, following a string of ignominious failures. And each of these men in their own way became the greatest leader their nations had ever known.

At the installation service for my first pastorate, I received a framed portrait of Abraham Lincoln from my then district superintendent of the organization from which I was ordained. It read:

## PERSERVERANCE

He FAILED in business in '31.
He was DEFEATED for State Legislation in '32.
He tried another business in '33, it FAILED.
His fiancée died in '35.
He had a nervous BREAKDOWN in '36.
In '43 he ran for Congress and was DEFEATED.
He tried again in '48 and was DEFEATED again.
He tried running for the Senate in '55, he LOST.
The next year he ran for Vice President and LOST.
In '59 he ran for the Senate again and was DEFEATED.
In 1860, the man who signed his name A. Lincoln was elected the 16th President of the United States.

*"The difference between history's boldest accomplishments, and its most staggering failures is often, simply, the diligent will to persevere."*
*– A. Lincoln*[8]

I never knew when I received this, how many times I would stop to read and re-read what was written on this framed portrait of Abraham Lincoln as it hung on my office wall. Every time I questioned myself and looked at my own failures, even though Lincoln's was a different kind of failure, I was still encouraged to keep going and not give up. I had to keep moving forward. In spite of my failures, God still wanted to do a work in me and through me. If I gave up, I would never accomplish the plan that God had for my life.

You cannot give up on yourself. Others may have given up on you, but they don't have the privilege or power to make you do the same. I have often retold a story shared with me about Winston Churchill. It is told that he was invited back to his grammar school after the war to speak to the graduating students. He was introduced with great fanfare and a

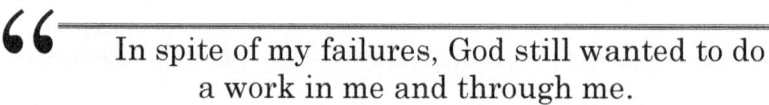

> In spite of my failures, God still wanted to do a work in me and through me.

long testimony of his formidable accomplishments. It was followed by a deep silence as the students sat in awe and in eager anticipation of the great words and stories that this famous hero and leader would share. Churchill slowly rose from his seat and walked to the podium, looked out at the audience and then began his speech. He proceeded very slowly and deliberately and said, "Never, never, never, never, never (seventeen times), never, never, never give up." He then turned from the podium and walked back to his seat and sat down. It is not failure that makes or breaks a person, but how one responds to it. If you can learn from your failures, if you can persist in spite of failure, if you can maintain a positive attitude, a forward-looking approach, and stand up again, then you will succeed in life no matter how many times you may fail.

This is where the starting line begins for you. I am sensitive to how bad it may look from your perspective right now. If you're sitting in a jail cell, have lost your job, have been kicked out of your home, are looking at divorce papers or you're thinking about just ending it all, I want you to take a deep breath and know that this is the beginning of

>  It is not failure that makes or breaks a
> person, but how one responds…

something new. A new journey and a new lease on life - an opportunity to have a renewal within your life. I would be honored to start this journey with you and wish to do so by praying this prayer with you as you make it your own:

*Lord, I come before you in my nakedness and shamefulness. I ask that you guide me as I take responsibility for my own actions; help me to forgive those who rejoiced in my failure, those who turned away from me and those who aided in compounding my own misery. Lord, help me to see them through Your eyes and feel for them with Your heart, for my own heart struggles with forgiveness. I pray You will forgive me for all the pain and hurt I have created. Help me to be the vessel You created me to be. Renew in me a right spirit and open my heart and mind to receive the wisdom and guidance I need. I plead Your blood over my life and I will do my best to trust in You as You once again begin anew in my life. In Jesus name I pray, Amen.*

Congratulations, you have now begun a new journey and what lies before you throughout these pages are words of encouragement, instruction, and prayer. My desire is that as you read, these pages will flow with compassion, discernment, and the fire of the Holy Spirit as the Lord moves you from the pit of your failure into the perfect plan He has already preordained for your life.

20 Broken

# Chapter Two
## What We Do In Secret Are Seeds Planted in Our Souls[9]

*"Humpty Dumpty sat on a wall.
Humpty Dumpty had a great fall.
All the king's horses and all the king's men
Couldn't put Humpty together again!"*[10]

We remember this fairy tale of Humpty Dumpty recited to us as children. We envision this fragile being shaped in the form of an egg, wobbling on the edge of a wall, when all of a sudden he falls and is broken into many pieces. The king sends out his horses and men, but the damage is too great and nobody can put him back together again.

When you take a look at the complexities of our nature, the war

> ...we too often find ourselves on the wall of life, attempting to have it both ways.

of flesh against spirit – we too often find ourselves on the wall of life, attempting to have it both ways. I wonder how many times Humpty Dumpty sat on the wall before the great fall happened? This tale tells us that they tried to put him together again! He must have had minor falls before, but nothing that had ever left him in a state of hopelessness before. I wonder what happened this time? What was it that caught his attention, enticing him to lean toward that thing, causing him to roll right over the edge?

Now, take this cute little rhyme and look at your own life. You are a fragile being created by the King of Kings and Lord of Lords.[11] You have attempted to straddle the wall, believing you are strong enough, talented enough, and too well connected to fall – at times you may even have considered yourself invincible. Yet, at this moment you might well be lying in your own mess, wondering why and how you have fallen into such sin. You look at your past, and as you reflect, you can see the warning signs at critical points in your life. The minor slips and falls you had before. The signs you ignored, signs that you thought did not apply to you. Yet you have come to this point where you have realized that the decisions you make now are more critical than the ones you made prior to your fall.

As I reflected on my failure, I wondered, where did it begin for me? As a young child, I had an insecurity within myself and a notion that I had to compete with my brothers for the affection of my parents. It brought forth an insatiable hunger to be needed, loved and praised by my parents. This lack of self-esteem in my young life led me down a dangerous path. My misapplied desire for the attention of my parents created within me a drive to do whatever I felt necessary to gain their attention. I would push the envelope, and at times I crossed the line by doing the wrong things for all the right reasons. I allowed myself to be deceived into believing that the ends justified the means. I would always justify in my own mind that I was fulfilling a need; they won't miss it; or we deserved it more than them, amongst other reasons I conjured in my own mind.

At twelve years old, I was responsible for the weekly grocery shopping for our family of six. I would take the money my father gave me for grocery shopping as he dropped me off at the super market. I would go into the store with a goal to purchase everything my mother wrote on the list, along with a few extras, always striving to hand my father back as much money as possible. It was an impossible task, unless I crossed a line. And that I did! I would change prices on food packages in the supermarket that in turn often cut the costs of the groceries in half.

I would then take all the coupons we had previously cut out at home, choosing the cash register of a cashier I knew. I would push that person to take my stack of coupons, regardless of the fact that very little, if any, in that stack represented what I had in my shopping cart. I would walk out of the store with bundles of groceries and change left over, excitedly awaiting the praise of my parents. Like an addict, each week I would work harder in order to receive a greater feeling of praise.

When questions were asked, I spoke in half-truths and at times, told my "little white lies," explaining that all those coupons were willingly accepted. Week after week I would attempt to outdo the previous week by purchasing more food, hoping to give back even more money to my father. I basked in the praises I received and cherished the glee my mother expressed when all the groceries were being unloaded into the fridge and the cupboards. In those moments, my addiction to be loved and needed was temporarily fulfilled.

These unethical and illegal actions set a pattern in my life that would eventually push me over the edge of that wall. Scripture clearly tells us,

> ...the decision to break the law or cross a moral line does not happen all at once.

"A little leaven, leaveneth the whole lump."[12] We always start off small – most often, the decision to break the law or cross a moral line does not happen all at once. It begins with one little lie; sneaking one little drink; taking that one thing not noticed; or some other questionable action. Irrespective of what that initial failing might be, it all eventually boils down to giving up on moral values and principles that are expected by our society and more importantly, our God.

What most often happens is that one will allow their own reasoning to create excuses to justify inappropriate actions that, through the course of time pushes one over that wall. You swayed back and forth and eventually leaned back one too many times, resulting in that one final incident that had you leaning back too far... you lost your balance and now find yourself broken. It is our good character and integrity that will always keep us grounded. The moment these attributes are removed, our lives become unstable. You may not have realized it, but you stopped paying attention to the important details that spoke to your character; you ignored those who told you they don't believe you because you lied one time too many; or a family member who said they can't trust you anymore – because you've stolen from them for the last time! Whatever the issue, these were the cracks in your façade, the minor falls you had in the past. However, this time you know it is different. The previous falls were in the form of situations that did not bring about a catastrophic event. Rather, they were little bumps in comparison. They were just a few nicks, bruises, and cracks, but nothing that kept you down.

In fact, there are many "little" things done in secret and never revealed or simply not considered a problem at the time. What we do in secret are the seeds that are planted in our souls and will remain covered for a season. Failure is the result of building on those successes we achieve

> Failure is the result of building on those successes we achieve through manipulation.

through manipulation. By manipulating the parameters of fair play, we are pushed into those gray areas of life, which quickly take root. There may well be initial successes, but these are soon overcome by the tangled creepers of sin we have allowed into our overall game plan or business strategy. Eventually, over time, the character flaws break through into the open areas of one's life for all the world to see.

This is the fall that is then seen as catastrophic. It is the one that breaks you and shatters everything you are. Then the story of Humpty Dumpty comes back to mind. Life at this moment is considered hopeless. No one can put you back together again. Thankfully, the Humpty Dumpty rhyme is only a fairy tale. We live in a very tangible world and in the knowledge of this reality comes forth a hope for something better. In this very real world we are presented with the ability and opportunity to pick up the pieces and move forward.

It takes time, patience, and an understanding of how you arrived at this broken state. In diagnosing your own situation with a laser-driven truth, you can begin to move forward and learn the valueable lessons which strengthen you in a way that will prevent such failures from being repeated in your life. But to reach this point, you need to take a moment right now to honestly reflect upon each decision and action you have taken that birthed this failure.

26 Broken

# Chapter Three
## Turning Regrets Into Positive Action[13]

*"When one door closes, another opens;
but we often look so long and so regretfully upon the closed door that we
do not see the one which has opened for us"*
**– Alexander Graham Bell**

Regrets can become a paralyzing force when they are not used as building blocks for positive change. Consider again the analogy of a stone thrown into a still pond that in turn creates ripples, one after another. You cannot suddenly still the pond. Even if you dive in and retrieve the stone, the water has already been stirred. In other words, "if only" will never change what has already

> You can live a life of regret, but that will never change the "if only's" of life.

been done. Too often, immediately after the failure has taken place or been revealed, we start thinking, "if only I didn't do that ... if only I had listened ... if only I could go back and change it!" You can live a life of regret, but that will never change the "if only's" of life. In fact, too often our shame – and the litany of "if only's" that follow – is a result of being caught and not necessarily due to what we have done wrong.

Whether you stand before a judge in a criminal or civil court or stand before a spouse, family member, or friend, it is the same with them as it is with God – they all want to see genuine remorse, not a fabricated story or crocodile tears. Are you truly sorry for what you did wrong?

The Biblical definition of repentance essentially relates to changing your mind.[14] True repentance involves a change of mind that results in a change of action.[15] Repentance is often linked to salvation, which includes a call to any individual to change their mind from rejection of Christ to faith in Christ.[16]

Repentance always involves a change of mind, whether it is repentance from a willful rejection of Christ or repentance from an ignorance or disinterest in Him. In broader terms, repentance relates to changing your mind about how you live, due to your faith in Christ. This includes a change of mind that causes a change in your subsequent actions. True Biblical repentance is expressed through a change in behavior. Hence, John the Baptist's call for people to produce fruit in

> Genuine repentance is demonstrated when one turns away from actions...

keeping with repentance.[17] Turning away from sin is an important step toward achieving true repentance. However, this must be followed by the cultivation of spiritual fruit which reflects the behavioral change experienced through being repentant. Genuine repentance is demonstrated when one turns away from actions that are in opposition to God's law. For example, when one repents of cheating, stealing, or committing adultery, they are no longer participating in that action or activity. When I was in junior high school, I was in a car with a bunch of friends and we were driving around the school grounds harassing a group of athletes. Yelling at them, cursing, and taunting them by pretending we were about to drive into them. We rationalized that it was all in fun and a fairly common prank. The following day, the phone rang in my home and it was the vice-principal. He began to yell at me, and right at that moment my father walked in and asked who it was. I told him and he took the phone from me and listened. He said a few words to the vice-principal and hung up the phone. At that moment, as a fifteen year old, I just knew that my life was over. I was dead!

My dad said, "Well… ?" So I told him I wasn't the one driving, and he said, "It doesn't matter!" In my attempt to get out of my perceived death sentence, I said, "I wasn't the only one in the car!" His eyes narrowed and his hands closed into fists as he once again said, "It doesn't matter." As I took a step back, I said, "But Dad, I wasn't the one swearing." His voice dropped even lower as he growled, "It doesn't matter." In an attempt to try and wiggle my way out of this doomed situation, my voice crackled and pitched as I said, "But Dad, there were nine of us jammed into the car, why did he have to pick me out? I mean, everyone does it to the jocks!" He moved toward me, placed one hand very firmly on my shoulder and in a very quiet, yet strong voice said, "You're not everyone!" He then turned away and walked out of the room. I stood frozen, waiting for the aftershock, for his return and the words: "You're grounded for the next twenty years," or his backhand… but nothing came. It was in those moments standing there in fear and reflecting on what just took place that it dawned on me. I'm not supposed to be like everyone else. My actions did not represent who I was supposed to be. Because I was with them and participating in those actions, I was just as guilty as the rest of my friends and just as responsible for all that had transpired.

In that revelation, I was embarrassed and ashamed because I did not represent who I was, the son of my father. I let him down. He was on the school building committee for the new high school. He was well known and respected, and his job was that of the Ombudsman for the Governor of our State. I realized that I needed to make changes in my behavior. I began by taking responsibility for my actions. I went to school and apologized to the vice principal. I changed my friends and began getting involved in productive activities. I wanted my Father to know that I understood what he meant and that I was truly remorseful for my behavior. I wanted to become what I was supposed to be and not be like everyone else.

>  ...it is not only apologizing for what you did wrong, but also accepting responsibility...

**CONSIDER THIS POINT: YOUR ACTIONS SPEAK LOUDER THAN YOUR WORDS!**

Remorse is an action word that moves you to be repentant. When you repent, it is not only apologizing for what you did wrong, but also accepting responsibility for your actions. If possible, you then do whatever is within your means to make it right. And throughout this process you change your behavior to ensure that you don't repeat such actions again.

Consider the analogy previously referenced concerning a stone thrown into a still pond that in turn creates ripples, one after another. You cannot suddenly still the pond. Even if you dive in and retrieve the stone, the water has already been stirred. In other words, "if only" will never change what has already been done.

What you must do first, is to take a look at the ripples in the pond of your life. The moment your failure – or more accurately, sin – was cast by you into the center of your life, the ripples then flowed outwardly, and as a result have had, and will continue to have, a direct impact first on those closest to you: your family, friends, neighbors, and co-workers. Shocked by the first ripple, disappointed when the next ripple hits, each progressive ripple brings with it feelings of betrayal, loss of trust, anger, and even hatred as these precious people are shaken by your actions.

And then there is a view from the side of the pond. From there, you see those connected to your family – friends, neighbors, and co-workers – they look on and spend their time thinking about your family and questioning their integrity as a result of your actions, or they observe your family and friends with pity because you're related to or close to those who they know. As a result of your failure, it is the individuals closest to you who become the collateral damage. They are the ones who experience undeserved shame and embarrassment because of your failure. It is little wonder that some people are so quick to disown – or disassociate themselves from the lives of – those who have experienced a spectacular public failing. As I reflect on my own failure, I immediately think of my twin brother and what he had to deal with emotionally because of the looks and whispers of others as they saw him. Did they question if he was just like me? Because we look so much a like, we are often mistaken for the other – how did my failure reflect upon him? Talk about collateral damage and the regrets I had because of what he had to go through because of me! Those who have allowed temptation to transform their actions into acts of sin have in turn manifested their own failure, and now they find themselves broken.

Take a moment to consider an Old Testament story about a righteous man named Job. Remember, he was righteous. He did not sin, fail his family, friends or God. In fact, God loved him and regarded him highly. When Satan came before God and challenged him about humanity, God

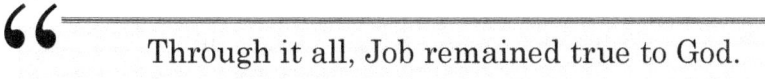

> Through it all, Job remained true to God.

asked Satan if he had considered Job. God then gave him permission to do whatever he wanted to Job, except kill him. Satan was unleashed to attack Job. Job lost all his possessions and wealth. His children were killed, and then his body was covered in boils and sores. Through it all, Job remained true to God. Yet in the midst of all the bad he went through, his friends – who we would expect to be there for him and to help him – kept their distance and wondered what evil he had done. His wife, probably embarrassed by the predicament they were in and angry for the loss of her children and wealth, told her husband that he should just curse God and die!

Now, allow me to put this into perspective. Job was a righteous man.

Through no fault of his own, no indiscretion, no sin, he was judged by his peers and in their moment of judgment they removed their trust in Job and stayed away from him. Then to add insult to injury, his own wife who was fed up with the situation just wanted her husband to curse God and die.[18] Yet, in the end, God restored all Job lost and more. The point I want to challenge you with is this: for those of us who have acted unrighteous and sinned, how much more will the actions of those around us be justified by our failure? Irrespective of whether or not they call themselves Christians or simply "good decent folk," their reaction to our sin will not differ from the reaction of Job's friends. In comparison, in a non-biblical sense, those who have judged us have had a solid reason to do so. If Job, who was righteous, could be vilified for a failure he had not brought upon himself, then I cannot claim "foul play" and shout back "hypocrite" to those who have responded negatively to my failure. In fact, do not be surprised to see the judgment of those around you magnified a hundred-fold in comparison to Job's situation.

Whether we like it or not, that is the cost of doing business with sin.

> You are already positioning yourself for a miracle from heaven…

People will always talk, but some thrive on the gossip associated with the negative aspects of other people's lives. It's bad enough that you are consumed with regret, but the truth is, you will also have to deal with gossipmongers snipping at you behind fake smiles. The one vital truth you can cling to is that you are already positioning yourself for a miracle from heaven as you work on turning your regrets into positive action. Take hold of the counsel offered through these pages. Keep your heart and mind centered on Christ, and as you act upon each recommendation you will see how your regrets become a steppingstone for positive actions in your life.

## Your Thoughts...

# Chapter Four
## Moving Past Your Failure- How God's Servants Did It[19]

*"For a just man falleth seven times, and riseth up again: but the wicked shall fall into mischief."*
**– Proverbs 24:16 (KJV)**

What mental image do people create when they consider the term: "a just man"? Most people probably think of a man who is righteous and of strong character. So to include in the same sentence the concept of righteousness and the concept of failure (a just man falleth seven times) creates a somewhat jarring picture. The two terms appear to be incompatible. Yet this scripture in the Book of Proverbs demonstrates that good people can fail, yet God calls on us to stand right back up when we do fall.

> These are the days that you may wonder if there really is any hope...

There are days that you may wonder if there really is any hope in the future. Will you really have another chance to make things right and move forward? During my own time of failure, when I considered some of the key leaders in the Bible who failed God, yet were reconciled to Him and were mightily used by Him, I knew there was hope for me and that God would see me through.

Let me demonstrate this point by sharing with you examples of three men in the Bible who failed God:

**King David**

Consider the story of King David. He was a warrior, psalmist, musician, and also a man after God's own heart.[20] Despite all of these titles, he had a moral failure that should have knocked him out of the will of God permanently and destroyed his standing with the people of Israel.

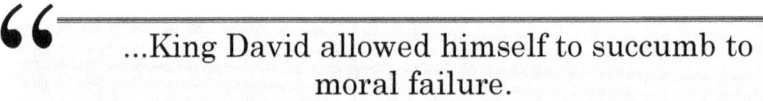

> " ...King David allowed himself to succumb to moral failure.

Yet David is recorded as one of the greatest kings in Biblical history who, in his own heart, was continually striving to emulate the heart of almighty God. The second Book of Samuel[21] records the situation in which King David allowed himself to succumb to moral failure. David was supposed to be on the battlefield with his men, yet we find him on the roof of his palace in the early evening. He sees a beautiful young woman named Bathsheba and, being the king, he uses his position to call this woman into his presence.

Having her presented to him is the second step David took along the path to failure. The first was to shirk his duty on the battlefield. The successive steps he took led to adultery and culminated in murder. Perhaps he was merely intrigued by her beauty and wanted simply to meet her and express his admiration. Perhaps King David did not plan to commit any sin, but if truth be told, his adulterous liaison with Bathsheba would not have taken place if the king had been out on the battlefield with his men. **As is the case with sin, it has its consequences.** Scripture informs us that a child was conceived by Bathsheba, who sent word to the king that she was carrying his baby. David's first reaction is an attempt to cloud the issue by covering his sin. David called Bathsheba's husband, Uriah, from the battlefield, telling him to go home and rest with his wife. David, of course, was expecting Uriah to have intercourse with his wife, removing the questionable issue of a child conceived in his absence.

Unfortunately for the king, Uriah was a loyal captain who set a warrior's example for his men. Uriah slept at the door of the king's house, unwilling to enjoy the comforts of home when his men were in the process of waging war. Becoming desperate, David attempted to make Uriah drunk so he would capitulate and be with his wife, but that did not work either. Notice how each step becomes progressively more desperate as David scrambles to cover his sin.

King David finally crossed a line that could not be erased. He sent Uriah to the front line on the battlefield, knowing there was a good chance he would be killed by the enemy in that vulnerable position. David thought he had finally succeeded in covering his sin when Uriah was killed in battle. David's actions, however, caused some other good men to die alongside Uriah that day. The king's adultery culminated in the multiple murders of his soldiers, all done in an attempt to hide his

> ...the actions we take to cover our guilt often have further repercussions.

initial sin.

In David's attempt to cover up what he had done wrong, innocent people had to pay the price. This is what happens when we fail and refuse to take ownership of our sin. In an attempt to hide our sin, the actions we take to cover our guilt often have further repercussions, causing people around us to become collateral damage. Those closest to us are hurt and wounded, if not worse, as a result of our actions.

Consider this point: David was the king of Israel. He could have done whatever he wanted to do. He could have rewritten the laws of the land to fit his own agenda. He had the ultimate veto power and could create any law he desired as king. Yet, there was a civic responsibility to which he was bound. King David had a moral obligation which called upon Godly principles he had to live by and did not have the right to disregard.

A person may be able to hide their failure from the public, but it is never hidden from God.

The prophet, Nathan, was sent by God to present this sin before David. When Nathan revealed to David that God knew of his sin, the king realized that even though he had authority over all the land, he could not rise above a moral authority. David knew that even if he rewrote the law of the land, giving him the privilege of having any woman he desired, it would go directly against God's law. David was at a crossroad. He could have denied his actions! He could even have categorically stated: "I did not have sexual relations with that woman!" But David's response is what made him a man after God's own heart. He spoke the simple truth: "*I have sinned against the Lord.*"[22] David took full responsibility for his

> David took full responsibility for his actions and did not offer any excuses.

actions and did not offer any excuses. This is what is expected of each individual when they fail. Going by the example of King David, people should take responsibility for their actions, and in requesting mercy, accept the consequences.

The consequences of my own actions resulted in me paying back money I did not personally benefit from at all. The funds I used (to buy groceries as a form of compensation for a struggling employee) had to be paid back to the organization I worked for, as well as the funds that were misappropriated. In all, it amounted to more than forty thousand dollars! Some people who know my story seem to think this was too heavy a price to pay, considering the money never went into my pocket. But, like King David, there were consequences to my sin. **Sin is the only stock that guarantees you a return which is greater than your investment.** The Apostle, Peter, also had his share of failures, which we will now examine in more detail:

**The Apostle Peter**

Peter's life serves as an excellent illustration of how ordinary people who have failed are used by God to accomplish great things. It was only by the grace of God that Peter could overcome his failures.

American writer, Dennis Waitley, puts this concept into perspective with a wise quote: "Failure should be our teacher, not our undertaker!"[23]

> " Failure should be our teacher, not our undertaker!

This is what Peter was able to learn through the grace of a loving God. Looking at Peter's life, we notice a string of failures. In each of these blunders, his intention is to improve his relationship with Christ, yet his failings occur as a result of him taking his eyes off Jesus. In each instance, Peter's human weakness is revealed in his attempts to relegate Christ's divinity to his own human understanding.

In the darkness of early morning,[24] walking across the sea of Galilee, Jesus approached His disciples. When Peter realized it was Jesus walking on the water, he asked Jesus to confirm His identity by calling Peter to Him, which Jesus readily did. Peter began walking upon the water until he took his eyes off Jesus, noticing how "boisterous"[25] the wind was, and so he started sinking into the water. **In spite of his failure, Peter is still the only recorded human being to walk on water – apart from Jesus,** who was both man and God. Another example of Peter trying to fit Christ's divinity into his own human perception came about after Jesus began giving His disciples an idea of how He would die, and the suffering He would endure. Peter's all-too-human response is to deny what he considers to be bad news. Peter rebukes Jesus, telling Him: *"this shall not be unto thee."*[26] The response Jesus gives to Peter is indicative of how quickly our human temperament vacillates between spirit and flesh.

Just prior to Peter's rebuke, Jesus commends him for being open to the Father's revelation that Jesus is "the Christ, the Son of the living God."[27] Jesus pronounces Peter blessed because "flesh and blood" have not revealed this to him, but rather His Father "in heaven."[28] Shortly after this, in response to Peter's rebuke, Jesus rebukes Peter in turn, explaining to him that he "savourest not the things that be of God, but those that be of men."[29] Peter slides, in a few verses, from receiving the proclamation that "upon this rock"[30] Jesus will build His church, to being exposed for

> " This vacillation between Spirit and flesh is a recurring theme...

basing his thoughts on the vagaries of the flesh rather than the truth of the Spirit. This vacillation between Spirit and flesh is a recurring theme in Peter's walk with Christ.

Yet another example is when Peter wrongly compared Jesus with mere mortal men.[31] When Jesus was transfigured before three of His disciples on a mountain, Peter was too quick to classify Him in the same category as Moses and Elias, offering to build "three tabernacles"[32] for them. God Himself had to rebuke Peter on this occasion, saying to him: "This is my beloved Son, in whom I am well pleased; hear ye him."[33] In other words, "Stop talking, Peter, and listen!" Time and again, Peter's brash and impulsive nature leads him into wrongful thoughts and wrong actions. He initially refuses to allow Jesus to wash his feet, relenting only when Jesus says to him, "If I wash thee not, thou hast no part with me."[34] Peter also slept through an extremely important prayer meeting in the Garden of Gethsemane, allowing his flesh to override his spirit yet again.[35] Jesus said to him on this occasion, "Watch and pray, that ye enter not into temptation: the spirit indeed is willing, but the flesh is weak."[36] Another failure includes Peter cutting off the ear of Malchus, the servant of the high priest, when a mob arrived to arrest Jesus.[37]

Perhaps his greatest failing, or at least, the one for which he was probably most remorseful, was on the night of Jesus' trial, when Peter denied any association with Jesus whatsoever.[38] After Jesus was crucified, Peter essentially quit his ministry and returned to fishing.[39] Of course,

>  He readily forgave Peter, reinstating him to the position he had originally been elevated.

Jesus was willing to overlook Peter's human weaknesses and failings. Jesus Himself personally experienced the myriad temptations faced by human beings on a daily basis. He readily forgave Peter, reinstating him to the position he had originally been elevated to as the rock upon which the Church of Christ would be built.[40] Peter's final failing recorded by scripture for our benefit was the hypocritical manner in which he would eat with the Gentile converts, but not in the presence of other Jews, for fear of the Jews.[41] The thing about compromise is that others, who look to their fellows for leadership, are sometimes led astray due to this compromise. Barnabas is a case in point, for we are told that he "also was carried away with their dissimulation."[42]

**In spite of Peter's many failings, after every failure, he dusted himself off and stood up again.** As a result of Peter's faith – not his failures – God used him to speak a message on the Day of Pentecost that changed the lives of three thousand people after delivering one sermon.[43] Jesus illustrates through Peter His long-suffering toward us. God is not focused on your failures as much as He is focused on operating through your faith.

There are many other people mentioned in scripture that could be used to illustrate how God restores and works through human beings in spite of their failures. However, one final illustration should suffice in making these points clear. We will now delve into the life of Samson.

## Samson

It has been more than three thousand years since the recorded death of Samson. Yet, Samson continues to be glorified and glamorized in

Hollywood movies. It was in the depth of his despair and failure that Samson achieved victory over the Philistines. Samson teaches us that even in the darkest days and loneliest times, it is still not too late to have a turnaround. It was when Samson surrendered his life to God, that he was restored before God.

Samson's biggest struggle was his desire to be seen as an angel in all he did, but to continue playing like the devil. You cannot have it both ways. Samson tried to live for God, but his actions betrayed the intentions of his heart. His ego and pride is what drove him into a spirit of arrogance. The Biblical depiction of Samson's story reveals his arrogance, especially the manner in which he flaunts his God-given attribute of immense strength, eventually allowing Delilah to prise from him that as long as Samson did not cut his hair, his strength from God would remain. **Too often, a person's title, position, or talent produces a spirit of entitlement.** Have you ever heard some prestigious personality make the statement, "Do you know who I am?" It is simple arrogance which leads an individual with humble beginnings to later tout their position or title as an excuse for their actions.

Chapters thirteen through sixteen of the Book of Judges tells The story of Samson's rise and his fall. This story speaks about the exploits that brought Samson, who was blessed by God, into a backslidden state. There are a few points to consider about Samson. They include his miraculous birth – his mother was barren until the angel of the Lord appeared and promised her a son.[44] Samson was declared by God to

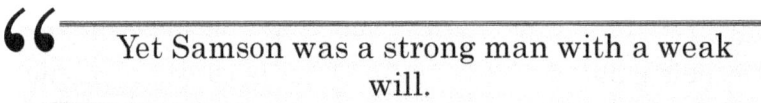

> Yet Samson was a strong man with a weak will.

be a Nazarite[45] from birth. God chose him to be a leader in Israel, one who would "begin to deliver Israel out of the hand of the Philistines."[46] Yet Samson was a strong man with a weak will, who continued to fail through his disobedience.

When Samson revealed to Delilah that his source of strength came from God through his Nazarite vow, it was his final act of disobedience,

> ...God never turned away from him, even though he disobeyed God in many ways.

one in which he essentially gave himself over to the Philistines to be tortured and humiliated. The lesson we can take from Samson's story is that God never turned away from him, even though he disobeyed God in many ways. His hair, which was an outward symbol of his inward devotion to God,[47] "began to grow again after he was shaven."[48] Samson may have failed on a personal level, but when his hair grew back and his strength returned, he accomplished what God had set out for him to do – he began the deliverance of "Israel out of the hand of the Philistines."[49] Ultimately, his failure did not define his relationship with God. His failure introduced him to the humility necessary to accomplish the task set out for him by God.

Samson's life is a clear illustration of how failure can still have adverse effects on our lives, even though God in His mercy brings us to a place of restoration in Him. Samson had to deal with his imprisonment and loss of site. Yet, after God restored Samson's strength, He honored Samson's request to "be at once avenged of the Philistines."[50] He used the gift of His God-given strength to bring judgment against the enemy of God's people, Israel.

There may be doors that are permanently closed as a result of your sin, but God in His love for you, will bring you out of that broken state. **The story of Samson demonstrates God's unconditional love for humanity.** How many times you fail is not important to God – whether or not you accept Jesus Christ into your life as Lord and Savior is what God focuses on. You may have the mark of your failure permanently scarred upon you, but you will also have the grace of God working in and through you as He brings you to a place of deliverance and restoration.

These three men exhibited several forms of failure that are common to humanity. Yet, in each situation, the moment they turned to God, He immediately began to work in them. He restored them to the exact place they needed to be for God to operate in and through them. The end result for King David was to be recorded in history as a man after God's own heart,[51] as well as becoming a vital link in the chain of lineage leading to the Messiah. Peter's spiritual legacy identifies him as the rock on which Christ would build His church. And Samson, who was assigned a task from before his birth, was used to bring deliverance for Israel, despite having failed miserably on a personal level.

Now, contemplate what God has in store for you and me. How will the end result of your failure bring glory to God while advancing His kingdom on the earth? God brought me to ..................... Now pray and let Him fill in the rest of your testimony!

## Your Thoughts...

46    Broken

# Chapter Five
## The Wisdom To Deal with Failure[52]

*"The only man who never makes a mistake
is the man who never does anything."*[53]
– **President Theodore Roosevelt**

The one qualifying factor that separates each individual referenced in Scripture who failed and was then restored, is that each of them did not allow their failure to define who they were. While other people may have believed the failure of these Bible characters would be permanent, the actual characters understood that through God's intervention and their obedience, they would be able to see past their failure, thus reducing it to a temporary setback. Failure is often a steppingstone to achieving the goals we set

> " Failure is often a steppingstone to achieving the goals we set out to reach.

out to reach. This is especially true when we consider ourselves through the eyes of a loving God. Biblical personas who succeeded in spite of an initial failing, took hold of the hope and grace extended to them by God, and transformed their moment of failure into an experience which ultimately brought them greater wisdom and eventual success.

As each one recovered, they used their failure as a tool for growth by learning from their errors and confessing it to God. As a result, they ended up being used by God in even mightier ways. The amazing proof of God's undying love for each of us in our failure is revealed in Paul's epistle to the Romans, where he writes, *"Moreover the law entered, that the offence might abound. But where sin abounded, grace did much more abound:..."*[54] Consider this powerful point: "where sin increased, grace increased all the more." This is the promise God gives to each of us. To deal with failure takes wisdom and maturity, especially if you plan to turn

> " To deal with failure takes wisdom and maturity,...

your situation around. Wisdom begins with understanding: Webster's dictionary defines failure as: "a state of inability to perform an expected function."[55] There is a Hebrew term, **Hatta**, that relates to the missing of a mark, goal or standard.[56] This definition is equivalent to sin. So, when we fail to meet God's standard, we have missed the mark He expects from us. We have failed God! When one sins against God, that person has failed to meet God's standard.

Wisdom tells us that failure must be addressed with a mature attitude. We can become successful in spite of our failure due to God's very credible grace and forgiveness. The following five steps are helpful in restoring the end-goal of success when they are applied to an initial failure:

1.) *Seek to use your failure as a lesson for growth and change. Failure reminds us of the consequences of our decisions.* **Failure shows us what we should and should not do.** Acknowledge your failure and refuse to hide behind trivial excuses. Confess any sin to God when sin is involved in the failure. This is in keeping with Scripture, as evidenced in John's gospel:

*"If we confess our sins, he is faithful and just to forgive us our sins, and to cleanse us from all unrighteousness."* – 1 John 1:9 (KJV)

2.) *Honestly and objectively examine what happened so you can learn from the failure. In the process, learn to put the failure behind you and move ahead*. Again, Scripture guides us through this process:

*"...forgetting those things which are behind, and reaching forth unto those things which are before..."* – Philippians 3:13 (KJV)

It is also very important to understand that there are different kinds of failure. Sometimes, according to the principles of Scripture, there are those who have genuinely failed. If you simply do not understand why you believe as you do, you will be unable to tell those who ask why you have placed your hope in Christ. Essentially, you will have failed in your responsibility to witness the truth of Christ to that person. Gaining understanding can become a steppingstone to becoming equipped and to being bold in your witness, but before you gained this understanding, you were experiencing failure. The first epistle of Peter puts this into perspective:

*"But sanctify the Lord God in your hearts: and be ready always to give an answer to every man that asketh you a reason of the hope that is in you with meekness and fear..."* – 1 Peter 3:15 (KJV)

> Believers can also be lured into a false sense of failure...

Believers can also be lured into a false sense of failure due to an incorrect view of success. Missionaries who labor faithfully in foreign countries may experience success in many areas, yet may not convert many people to Christ. This by no means indicates they are failures. The prophet, Isaiah, was sent by God to preach to a nation who would not listen. God even told him so beforehand (see Isaiah 6:8-10). To the nation of Israel, who heard Isaiah's message yet refused to repent, Isaiah may well have been classified as a failure, but in God's eyes he was a man who succeeded in the divine task given to him.

Personal failure can also be caused by the actions of others due to the way in which we respond. Scripture allows us to be angry at those who harm or hurt us, but we are commanded not to sin in spite of our anger. We are also told to put our anger aside when the day is done. A passage from Paul's epistle to the Ephesians makes this clear:

*"Be ye angry, and sin not: let not the sun go down upon your wrath..."*
– Ephesians 4:26 (KJV)

3.) ***Know the right measurement stick to determine failure or success before God.*** We cannot change yesterday, but what we do today determines what tomorrow will be like. The standard of measurement used by Christians to determine success and failure is an important part of becoming mature in their walk with Christ. The standards applied

> The standards applied by the world are not the standards of Christ.

by the world are not the standards of Christ. Most worldly beliefs about success that people apply to themselves and others are simply distortions of the truth.[57]

Most worldly ideas of success are based on some form of faulty comparison. **Failure is not based on whether others will forgive us, but whether or not we are able to forgive ourselves.** We must learn to love and forgive ourselves, much like our loving God extends His forgiveness to us.

4.) ***Scripture reveals the many ways in which we may fail God, while at the same time demonstrates how God never fails His people.*** Even Solomon, in all his wisdom, was enticed away from God when he grew old, by the gods of his wives.[58] But Yahweh (God) had mercy on Solomon for the sake of his father, David,[59] and *"for Jerusalem's sake,"*[60] which God had chosen. Yahweh literally spared Solomon the ignominy of having his kingdom torn away from him while he lived. In spite of Solomon going *"after Ashtoreth the goddess of the Zidonians, and after Milcom the abomination of the Ammonites,"*[61] and building a *"high place for Chemosh, the abomination of Moab, in the hill that is before Jerusalem, and for Molech, the abomination of the children of Ammon,"*[62] God still had mercy on him. Why? Why did God have mercy on Solomon? A verse in the First Book of the Chronicles sheds some light on this question:

*"And David said to Solomon his son, Be strong and of good courage, and do it: fear not, nor be dismayed: for the Lord God, even my God, will be with thee; he will not fail thee, nor forsake thee, until thou hast finished all the work for the service of the house of the Lord."* – 1 Chronicles 28:20 (KJV)

King David's relationship with God enabled God's protection of Solomon to be courteously extended to him, even though he no longer deserved God's protection. God's righteousness will not fail,[63] and neither will His compassion, which is renewed *"every morning."*[64] God is faithful! Once He gives His word, no force in heaven or on earth can change the outcome of what He sets in motion:

*"For as the rain cometh down, and the snow from heaven, and returneth not thither, but watereth the earth, and maketh it bring forth and bud, that it may give seed to the sower, and bread to the eater: So shall my word be that goeth forth out of my mouth: it shall not return unto me void, but it shall accomplish that which I please, and it shall prosper in the thing whereto I sent it."* – Isaiah 55:10-11 (KJV)

5.) ***Failure teaches us many important truths, but perhaps the most important lesson of all is the knowledge of how desperately we need God in our lives.*** Without His mercy and grace, human beings have no method of redemption after failure. Without God, failure becomes a pattern in our lives, even though we might not recognize the different types of failure we succumb to on a daily basis. The wisdom gained in understanding where we have failed becomes the very tool that enables our personal growth.

While the information above will be useful for an individual's personal journey, empowering them to deal with failure from a vantage point of increased knowledge, let me take a moment to expound upon appropriate ways of dealing with failure from a church leadership viewpoint. There are definite overlaps between the information needed for individual transformation and the information needed for church leadership when dealing with failure. However, while it is important for

> ... important for leadership teams to devise a standard method for dealing with failure.

church leadership to understand the process outlined above – so they can initiate these steps with church members who have failed – it is also crucially important for leadership teams to devise a standard method for dealing with failure. What follows is some practical advice from a group of pastors, interspersed with a few relevant details of my own experience, with specific regard to the way in which leadership handled my personal failure.

In October 2012, an article was published on what pastors had to say about moral failures within church leadership.[65] The pastors interviewed agreed that the first thing to do in the event of moral failure among church staff is to inform the congregation. The danger in trying to hide a moral failure often leads to rumors, which can be far more damaging than the truth.[66] As one pastor put it, "a public leader's failure deserves a public explanation."⁶⁷ Transparency is crucial to resolving the situation, as anything hidden will eventually surface, creating a loss of trust from the congregation's viewpoint.

After my personal failure, I went to my church board and explained to them what took place and how I had sinned. I asked that we hold a church business meeting so I could share my failure with the membership of the church. On the night of the meeting I told my wife I would request that a vote be taken as to my status within the church. I was willing to present my resignation or to be removed from my pastorate if this was the desire of the membership.

Only the complete truth will set people free. Now, that is not to say we should divulge all the sordid details of a sexual sin from the pulpit, but church members should be named, as well as the kind of sin in which they have indulged.⁶⁸ Of course, this should only be done once the guilty parties have been counseled, and an effort has been made to set them on

> ...the sins of those who have failed does not diminish anything these people have done...

the path to restoration. It must also be emphasized to the congregation that the sin of those who have failed does not diminish anything these people have done in ministry. Of course, this needs to be countered by the flip side of that particular coin: "the impact the person has had on people's lives doesn't diminish the seriousness of the sin."⁶⁹

Another aspect of restoration is the importance of retaining value within the staff and leadership of a church – or any organization for that matter. What this means is that time is better spent invested in restoring those who occupy positions necessary to the functioning of a church, rather than teaching another person from scratch. The wisdom gained by those who willingly repent and follow the path to restoration set out for them by the pastor will most likely stand that church in good stead down the line. We all have failed at some point in our lives, and having brothers and sisters nearby who are able to coach us through our failures will be of added benefit to the body of Christ.

It was because of my failure that I was able to truly appreciate and respect the sensitivities of my role as pastor and the protection of the membership. Unbeknown to the congregation, I had already told God that in the voting process, if there was a single vote in favor of me stepping down or being removed, that I would voluntarily resign. My mind was focused on the Scripture that announced how all the angels in heaven rejoiced over one sinner who repented (Luke 15:10).[70] Therefore, if just one person was that important to heaven, then so must I honor and affirm that point. The vote was unanimous for me to remain. However, I knew that I needed to work on addressing my personal failings. So I had the church membership vote in a senior pastor with full pastoral rights, while I focused on the repercussions pertaining to my failure.

Within any organization governed and attended by people, it is inevitable that moral failures among staff and leadership will occur from time to time, especially during periods of growth.[71] As an organization expands, the people involved expect the moral guidance of leadership to increase accordingly, but this is not always the case. The added pressure

> " ...the people involved expect the moral guidance of leadership to increase...

to perform at an increased pace or more stringent level of expertise must be balanced out, either by employing additional staff members to share the workload, or by implementing advanced training schedules for those fulfilling leadership roles.

Being prepared for failure is perhaps the best antidote to allowing the failure of a prominent leader to scandalize the entire organization. Believing it simply won't happen in your particular church or organization is unrealistic and shortsighted.

Knowing how to handle an individual's moral failure from an organizational standpoint allows for immediate action. Moral failure within church staff or leadership usually disqualifies the individual/s involved from ministry duties, at least for a time, during which a process of restoration can be followed. However – and this is a very important clarification – those who have failed must be willing to repent, and also to engage with church elders or leaders in the process leading to their restoration. Once the person experiencing failure has agreed to submit to church leaders, the concept of God's grace is of paramount importance. This process of "counseling, caring for the affected families, keeping the involved parties accountable, and continuously speaking into their lives could take years."[72] Some who have failed, especially if their failure is of a moral nature that becomes public, may not wish to be elevated back into the public eye. Even so, a good leader will encourage that person to at least undergo the process of restoration so their personal self-worth is boosted. Having gone through this process they may yet, in time, come to value and appreciate the lessons they are able to pass on to society.

The wisdom to deal with failure usually needs to be imparted to those who have failed. However, those leaders who are called upon to address failure are sometimes also in need of this wisdom. For leaders and those being counseled, it is important that each decision made and every step taken is applied in a manner that affirms Biblical precedents and requirements. Dealing with failure requires one step by the individual who has failed, then one step by the leader , and then back and forth throughout the process. It is important that each step is taken

> Dealing with failure requires one step by the individual...one step by the leader...

in good order, so it builds upon the previous steps taken. For example, encouraging one who has failed to apologize to the people they have hurt before establishing that they are willing to repent before God and to ask His forgiveness is counterproductive to the entire process. Of course, each set of circumstances will be unique, but generally speaking, none of the steps outlined in this chapter should be neglected. It also makes the best sense to follow these steps in the order set out in this chapter. The amount of time it takes an individual to move into a place of restoration will differ from person to person. Every individual's restorative process will be based on their personal circumstance, their commitment to God and their willing submission to His redeeming love. The Book of Proverbs sets out four prerequisite concepts for dealing with failure:

*"In all thy ways acknowledge him, and he shall direct thy paths. 7 Be not wise in thine own eyes: fear the LORD, and depart from evil."* – Proverbs 3:6-7 (KJV)

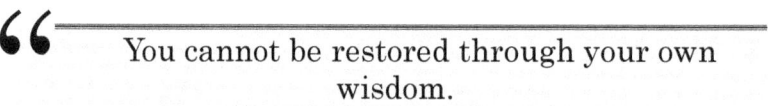

> You cannot be restored through your own wisdom.

You cannot be restored through your own wisdom. You need God and those godly individuals who care for you, and who are willing to counsel and guide you in grace and with authority. Consider the four concepts dealt with in the Scripture above. How does one go about acknowledging God in all your ways? In essence, this would mean you begin your day in prayer, followed by a time of meditation on the Word of God. Then, as you progress through your day, enacting the functions you have to perform, you would be in communion with the Holy Spirit, asking His advice before committing to any decisions you take.

It would also mean responding to all the people you deal with in a manner consistent with the love Jesus commanded us to show to one another. Basically, in all that you do, be aware of the Holy Spirit within you. **You could also keep the image in your mind of Jesus standing next to you as you walk through your day.** This will ensure that everything you think, say, and do, will reflect your acknowledgement of God, and will ensure that God will direct the daily paths you take.

Do not consider yourself to be wise, but rather thank God for the wisdom He has bestowed upon you. Nobody likes a vainglorious braggart, so walk humbly through life, especially when you excel at any given task. Point the glory back to God, who has blessed you with the ability to excel in those areas. Many people become confused when directed to *"fear the Lord,"* but the word, "fear" in this context relates

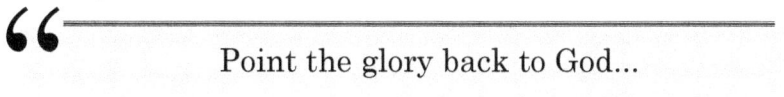

Point the glory back to God...

to reverence and respect. It also includes a sense of being apprehensive about failure when serving the Almighty God who created everything that exists, especially when failure is due to a casual approach.

Finally, it is up to us to make a conscious decision to depart from evil. This begins with controlling the thoughts that come into your mind. Chapter twelve goes into more details about this process of control that you can develop. **Departing from evil also involves a conscious decision not to allow your words or deeds to become caught up in any evil.** The children of God are commissioned with destroying evil wherever we may find it. Your failure has set you on the path of gaining this knowledge so you can ultimately turn it into experiential wisdom, directed by our Lord and Saviour.

# Chapter Six
## Finding God When Others Have Abandoned You[73]

*"And the Lord, he it is that doth go before thee; he will be with thee, he will not fail thee, neither forsake thee: fear not, neither be dismayed."*
– **Deuteronomy 31:8**

It is amazing how success shines like a glowing light at night which attracts many people, while failure is like a violent wind that blows the masses away. When failure arrives at your doorstep, you feel with keen disappointment the sudden abandonment of those you thought would be there. Just as there are tolls on many of our highways, so too are there tolls that must be paid on the road of life. Failure is often

> ❝ ...so too are there tolls that must be paid on the road of life.

linked to sin, especially moral failure. The cost of sin has to be paid for – it is one of God's universal laws affecting all humans. All too often, the result of sin is felt in the high cost of relationships – people naturally shy away from those experiencing the aftershock of a moral failure.

They somehow feel they will be tainted by the breakdown of the façade you have been holding up for them to see. Church elders and experienced leaders will sometimes guide and support you through this difficult time, but some will not. Sin always carries a cost – one you will pay regardless of how you arrived at that point.

As family and friends scatter away from that ditch you find yourself in, you begin to realize there is no way out of the hole you went ahead and dug for yourself. Of course, the depth of your despair will be relative to the specific aspects of your failure, but one thing is certain: it is impossible to lift yourself out of a moral failure by relying on your own ability. Trusting too confidently in your own ability is what caused you

> " Trusting too confidently in your won ability is what caused you to fail...

to fail in the first place! Trusting God and His Word is always a more reliable option, and although you may be realizing that now, you still need help to clamber out of that ditch of despair called failure. Surely someone must be willing to cast you a lifeline and extend you a helping hand?

Possibly, but that will depend on the relationships you have developed along the way. Most often, people respond to failure with judgment. They may say something like: "You made your bed, now lie in it!" While this may be true, you don't have to spend the rest of your life wallowing in a pit of despair. With God's help, you can use this failure as your personal steppingstone to success.

What must take place for you to rise out of that pit begins with trust. In my own experience, as I looked for someone I could trust that would help me, I found there were some who had the position and knowledge, but refused to extend any form of mercy or assistance. Then there were those who had the ability, yet their agenda was to inflict judgment rather than extend a hand of grace. I remember feeling hurt and then bitter as my trust in certain leaders was squashed, especially after realizing I no longer held any value in their eyes because of my failure. It was at this point I realized I had to trust someone who had the ability and the desire to help me. My wife and a few dear friends where there, but they could not do what I needed done. After encountering many cul-de-sacs, it finally dawned on me at the end of my road that God was simply waiting for me to trust Him for all my needs, my safety, and my future.

As I reflect on those dark days, I am able to see with hindsight that God's love for me is real. His best interest for me has always been at the heart of our relationship. I know this with positive certainty, as I have

> " His best interest for me has always been at the heart of our relationship.

experienced His grace and mercy firsthand. Just as God spoke comfort into the lives of the Jewish exiles in Babylon, so did He speak the same words of comfort to me in my day of despair:

*"For I know the thoughts that I think toward you, saith the Lord, thoughts of peace, and not of evil, to give you an expected end." – Jeremiah 29:11 (KJV)*

God never stopped thinking about His people. Even though Israel's sin and disobedience caused their downfall into slavery, God wanted them to know their plight would be remedied, but that they would have to stop trusting their own initiative and turn back to the God of their fathers. The verses following God's promise to bring their captivity to an end explain what is expected of Israel for this to take place:

*"Then shall ye call upon me, and ye shall go and pray unto me, and I will hearken unto you. 13 And ye shall seek me, and find me, when ye shall search for me with all your heart." – Jeremiah 29:12-13 (KJV)*

This Scripture speaks to all who have failed. God is saying the very same thing to you in your failure that He said to Israel in their time of distress. You simply have to call on Him and pray to Him, and He will hear you – when you earnestly search for God with all your heart, you will find Him. You will find that helping hand you were searching for extended towards you in mercy and forgiveness. This is the true hand that can restore you and transform the mess your life has become into a

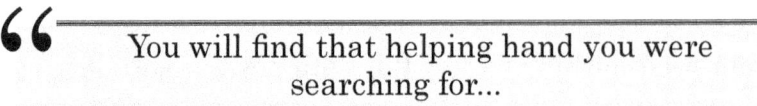
> You will find that helping hand you were searching for...

masterpiece of hope. A hope that will inspire others held captive by their failure.

King David was astonished at the extent and depth of God's plan for our lives. David understood such plans included the love, strength, and favor of God even before the moment of our conception. God's heart was filled with love for you before you were born, and His thoughtful contemplation of what would be best for you began at your birth. He will continue to lovingly consider you throughout your life's journey. David wrote about how tenderly God brings every human into being:

*"Thine eyes did see my substance, yet being unperfect; and in thy book all my members were written, which in continuance were fashioned, when as yet there was none of them." – Psalms 139:16 (KJV)*

Once you understand that God truly loves you and desires the best for you, it becomes easier to turn to Him. When you grasp the fact that God uses failure to hone people into sharper tools for His service, it becomes easier to run toward Him rather than away from Him during times of crisis. Simply put, you need to decide the direction you will take after being rejected by people due to your failure. Either way, you have a long and difficult road ahead of you. Choosing to accept God's grace and forgiveness assures you of a light at the end of the tunnel. Refusing God's help will most likely leave you nursing the bitterness of rejection for an indeterminate period of time, if not indefinitely. People often seek comfort in material indulgence when feeling rejected. Some turn to an over-indulgence in liquor, others indulge in comfort-eating, casual sex, or any other pastime that blankets their feelings of low self- esteem and shame. This is a form of self-sabotage that sinks the individual into an

> " People often seek comfort in material indulgence when feeling rejected.

ever-deepening downward spiral. So, knowing that turning to God is the most practical solution, how do we begin the process?

In one word – Worship!

Worship is the one sure-fire method that will keep the darkness from overwhelming you. Did you know that Job owned thousands of livestock, *"a very great household,"* and *"was the greatest of all the men of the east?"*[74] Bearing this in mind, consider Job's response to the news that he had just lost his oxen, asses, sheep, servants, camels, and all ten of his children: *"Then Job arose, and rent his mantle, and shaved his head, and fell down upon the ground, and worshipped..."*[75] All the solace you need will be found in worshipping God. **When all else has failed, worship the Lord.** [76] In spite of Job having lost just about everything of value to him, he worshipped the Lord. All that we are and all that we have comes from God, so even when it is taken from us we should still worship the Lord because none of it was ours to begin with.[77] That may be a difficult concept to accept, but it is the only one that makes any sense, at least from a spiritual perspective. Job was one of the few ancients to grasp this concept. Jesus pointed to the importance of true worship, knowing it is the only way to keep a clear channel open to the Father at all times:

*"But the hour cometh, and now is, when the true worshippers shall worship the Father in spirit and in truth: for the Father seeketh such to worship him. 24 God is a Spirit: and they that worship him must worship*

*him in spirit and in truth." – John 4:23-24 (KJV)*

Jesus knew the importance of true worship. The best way of finding solace in your hour of need is through worship, prayer, and by meditating on God's word. It is through communion with God that we are able to experience His grace and mercy, and it is through Scripture that this divine truth is given to us: *"Let us therefore come boldly unto the throne of grace, that we may obtain mercy, and find grace to help in time of need."*[78] Jesus' love for us is not just an emotional or sentimental feeling. His love for us is very real and effective when we know how to approach His throne. Jesus requires from us the same love in return, verified by our obedience to Him. John's gospel explains that the test of our love for Jesus should be reflected in our obedience to Him: "If ye love me, keep my commandments."[79] These are the words of Jesus to his disciples. Jesus generally kept things simple. It is we who complicate the processes of life.

The best thing that could've happened to me was the abandonment of others. What was meant to destroy me served only to sharpen my focus on my Lord and Savior, Jesus Christ. My trial of failure served to strengthen my relationship with Jesus. I learned how to have communion with Him through His Word and during my times of prayer. His mercy and grace was extended to me through my wife, my family, and a few close friends. They were my oasis in the middle of the desert. Through

> My trial of failure served to strengthen my relationship with Jesus.

Christ, they brought comfort and peace. When I was full of doubt and fear they spoke words of wisdom and encouragement. I knew God was using them to make sure I would not lose Him again.

When Jesus told Peter to step out of the boat and come toward Him, Peter stepped out in faith and began to walk on water.[80] The moment he took his eyes off of the Lord, he began to sink.[81] God's Word reminded me to keep my eyes on Him so I would not slip back into that ditch. It is often in your loneliest state – when your heart is desperate to feel Him – that your spiritual eyes can be opened to see Him.

To who else can you turn who will be there no matter what? He solemnly promises, *"I will never leave thee, nor forsake thee."*[82] Finding God did not mean I no longer experienced conflict or trouble. It meant that the peace I now had in Him was based on the knowledge and personal experience I had received through working on the process of overcoming my failure. One crucial aspect of the experiential knowledge I received is that God is the provider of everything we need.

> Finding God did not mean I no longer experienced conflict or trouble.

Through the blessings of God, I was able to miraculously pay back, within one year, the more than forty thousand dollars I owed to the organization I had been directing. God used people I knew and people I did not know, to bless me and meet my every need. Our bills were paid, and we always had food on our table. I was working, and slowly, over time, I began to minister again. Every need I had, God met with the gracious abundance only He can supply!

Another important lesson I learned while processing my failure is that the presence of misfortune is not necessarily the absence of God's grace.[83] In fact, people are sometimes used as the agents of our misfortune according to the will of God, for without certain trials and tribulations, we will not learn the lessons we need to learn to be of the best possible service to Him. Chapter Fourteen goes into more detail on this subject, explaining how Joseph overcame what initially seemed to be a terrible failure.

Joseph's brothers sold him into slavery, but the manner in which he processed this terrible betrayal allowed him to be mightily used of God in saving his family and many other Israelites from a dire famine. God's grace is always sufficient to meet every need arising in our lives... we simply have to trust His word.

Something else we need to understand is that God will sometimes use us to fill a position vacated by another person who has suffered a personal misfortune.[84] Similarly, we cannot begrudge those who may step in to fill our position after we have failed. We should rather bless them and encourage them to greatness in their new position, as this is the more gracious response, and we ultimately sow what we reap. The show must go on and we have to trust that God is in charge of our lives regardless of what the surface details might project. Blessing others while we face hardship is not only what Jesus expects of us, it is also a great way to reflect to others that you refuse to be defined by your failure.

While worship reveals to God your intention to trust Him with resolving your difficulties, prayer is an indication of what you think you require from God. Of course, God already knows what you need, but communication is a two-way process, and you need to express yourself to Him before He can respond accordingly. King David exemplified this principle when the child conceived in his adultery with Bathsheba lay dying. David prayed and fasted for seven days in the hope of deflecting

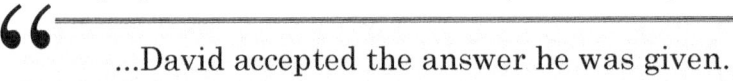

> ...David accepted the answer he was given.

the death of the child.[85] David continued to pray while waiting for an answer from God. When the child died, David accepted the answer he was given. Take note of David's response to the child's death:

*"Then David arose from the earth, and washed, and anointed himself, and changed his apparel, and came into the house of the Lord, and worshipped..." – 2 Samuel 12:20 (KJV) (Emphasis added)*

While there was yet hope, David prayed. When hope turned to personal tragedy, David worshipped. David accepted his failure – he admitted to the prophet Nathan that he had sinned against the Lord[86] – followed by prayer, fasting, and then worship, even though he did not receive the result for which he had prayed. Who knows what might have happened had David responded differently. Perhaps Solomon would not have been born. Perhaps God would have had to find an alternative bloodline through which His Son Jesus would be born. God is always able to turn failure into success. We simply have to use the tools at our disposal – worship, prayer, and the acceptance of God's grace.

There is a distinction between God's grace and His mercy. God's mercy embraces all of His creation,[87] while He extends His grace to those who put their faith and trust in Jesus.[88] While grace is connected to eternity, mercy is connected to our daily lives. [89] The Greek meaning of the word

> While grace is connected to eternity, mercy is connected to our daily lives.

"mercy" in the New Testament is eleos, which means: "kindness" or "compassion." The word eleos is "the outward manifestation of pity; it assumes need on the part of him who receives it, and resources adequate to the need on the part of him who shows it."[90] An excellent example of God's mercy toward humanity is found in the Book of Lamentations:

*"It is of the Lord's mercies that we are not consumed, because his compassions fail not. 23 They are new every morning: great is thy faithfulness." – Lamentations 3:22-23 (KJV)*

Even though we sin against God on a daily basis (disobedience, envy, lust, hatred etc.), He has mercy on us, allowing us to face another day. At the start of each new day He greets our weaknesses with fresh mercy. Grace, on the other hand, is linked to the concept of salvation.[91] Grace is

God's gift to us. We can do nothing to earn it, other than putting our faith in Jesus Christ:

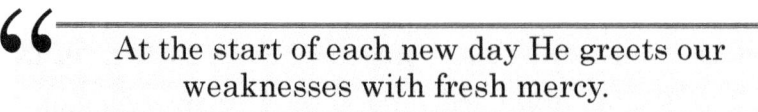

> At the start of each new day He greets our weaknesses with fresh mercy.

*"For by grace are ye saved through faith; and that not of yourselves: it is the gift of God: 9 Not of works, lest any man should boast."* – Ephesians 2:8-9 (KJV)

When we reach out to God in our time of need, He reaches out to us in turn.[92] Knowing this, it doesn't really matter who abandons or rejects us when we experience failure. We have a lifeline to God, who will always show us grace and mercy. Grace is when God gives us what we don't deserve and mercy is when God doesn't give us what we do deserve. [93] By following the Biblical call for worship, it is my earnest prayer and hope you will be able to find God when you need Him.

## Your Thoughts...

70   Broken

# Chapter Seven
## Finding Forgiveness Starts With You[94]

*"The rule is: we cannot really forgive ourselves unless we look at the failure in our past and call it by its right name."*
**– Lewis B. Smedes**

Forgiving yourself can be one of the most difficult and challenging processes you may experience after a failure. Feeling broken and beaten down, but trying to rise up from your bed of shame, you are suddenly swamped with remorse, overwhelmed by regret... and guilt, which turns to disgust when you look in the mirror. Forgiving yourself almost seems obscene. If you could go back and change things,

> **Forgiving yourself almost seems obscene.**

forgiving yourself would seem more appropriate, but this cannot be. So you refuse to forgive yourself. However, in order to move forward from your state of brokenness, forgiving yourself is a part of the process.

Remembering your humanity is the first step to regaining some perspective. The Bible explicitly informs us that, *"all have sinned."*[96] In fact, every one of us was born into sin, so we are not perfect, as much as we may strive for perfection. Recognizing our imperfect nature reminds us we will constantly be learning lessons throughout our lives. An Olympic gold medalist does not show up on the day of the competition to win the gold with no prior experience. No! That person had to put in a lifetime of practice. They had to learn from every mistake and improve on every positive aspect of their training schedule so they could become proficient enough to win the gold. Life is just like that. We learn from the good and the bad in our lives. When we mess up we can learn not

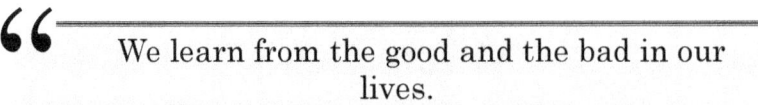
> We learn from the good and the bad in our lives.

to repeat the same error. If we desire to succeed, we keep honing and perfecting those elements which produce success. These successful elements on which we focus keep propelling us forward.

I remember feeling embarrassed when I was told I needed to forgive myself. I wondered how could I possibly forgive myself knowing the hurt I had inflicted on others. I found it easier to focus on the people who refused to forgive me – what right did I have to forgive myself? The very concept seemed absurd.

The beauty contained within human failure – if you can believe there is such a thing – is God's response to our human frailty. He wants to set us free from the guilt, regrets and self-disgust that we hold onto. **What has transpired is in the past. What is done, is done – both good and bad – this must be understood.** It is regret that keeps one living in the past. It is regret that ties your hands and will not allow you to pick up the pieces of your life. As spoken about in a previous chapter, regret, if used properly, can elicit positive behavior when it is used in the present to ensure that past mistakes are not repeated. Regret in this sense is encompassed within the essence of repentance, or showing remorse for your wrongdoing, which serves to prevent the same mistake occurring again. Displaying a contrite heart before God will earn you His favor.[97] God in fact goes so far as to say that He *"dwells"* with those *"of a contrite and humble spirit, to revive the spirit of the humble, and to revive the heart of the contrite ones."*[98] The International Bible Encyclopedia explains in detail the meaning of a contrite heart:

"A contrite heart is one in which the natural pride and self-sufficiency have been completely humbled by the consciousness of guilt."[99]

While regret can be used as a reminder to keep embracing repentance and contrition, harboring a deep-seated regret is counterproductive to moving on with your life. When you energize the negativity of regret by wallowing in your past failures, you become stuck. Over time this

> When you energize the negativity of regret by wallowing in your past failures...

leads to a self-destructive mindset. Such a mindset will sabotage your progress. Relationships cannot be healed due to feelings of self-doubt and unworthiness resulting from deep-seated regret. Harboring regret can cause you to label yourself by what you did rather than according to who you are in Christ, allowing depression to set in.

Hopelessness becomes your chief companion, and as previously mentioned, will in turn lead to varying forms of self-medication and other forms of self-induced addictions. The most drastic form of hopelessness sometimes ends in suicide. This drastic measure can be avoided if we accept the Word of God. In His Word, God tells us, *"My grace is sufficient for thee."*[100] Followed by this truth is the marvelous revelation: *"for my strength is made perfect in weakness."*[101]

## Your first step toward forgiving yourself is asking God to forgive you.

Again, you may say you are not worthy, but none of us are. This is why Christ died on Calvary's cross – to ensure we have a hope for tomorrow and a direct pathway to Him.

When you ask in all sincerity, God will forgive you! In your weakness, He will make you strong. As you begin to move forward in the process of dealing with your failure, you need to become bold in crying out for God's touch – much like the story told in Scripture of blind Bartimaeus.[102] Bartimaeus was a blind man who sat on the roadside begging when one day, he heard Jesus was approaching. He began to shout and call out to Jesus, but others told him to be quiet. Bartimaeus refused to be silenced, knowing he needed the power of Christ if he was to be a whole being. He shouted even more loudly to Jesus, saying: "Thou son of David, have

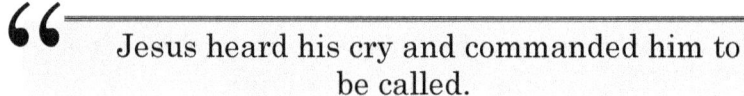

> Jesus heard his cry and commanded him to be called.

mercy on me."[103] Jesus heard his cry and commanded him to be called. When Bartimaeus was told that Jesus had called him, he threw aside his cloak, then rose up and went to Jesus. On that day, Bartimaeus asked to have his sight restored. Jesus honored his request, telling him his faith had made him whole. Bartimaeus immediately received his sight and Scripture tells us he *"followed Jesus in the way."*[104]

The miracle in this story is much more than the sight of a blind man being restored. The greater miracle is that this restoration transformed his whole life. He went from being a blind beggar to a man who could see and was now a follower of Christ. Jesus, in His mercy, He loves to give us more than we ask for. Bartimaeus just wanted to see, but God wanted his position in society to change! In one bold proclamation of his faith in Christ, Bartimaeus was changed from the social status as a cast away to becoming a follower of Christ.

Let me share with you the key points that produced such a miraculous transformation. The first thing blind Bartimaeus did was to call on the Lord. **This is what we must do in our brokenness – we must call on Him.** There will be those who tell you to be quiet, that you are underserving, that your own mistakes brought you to this place, and that you must just accept the status quo you have instigated. But notice that Bartimaeus did not listen to the bystanders. All he focused on was the fact that Jesus was passing by and he needed to attract His attention. The simple option would have been to agree with the label society had pinned on him: blind beggar. You too may choose to accept the label you have been pinned with. You may even agree it is by your own actions that you are labeled as such and it is with good reason you find yourself in this predicament. But this does not mean you have to wear that label indefinitely.

The second thing he did was cast away his cloak. Bartimaeus threw off the image or the title society had given him. That cloak represented his own brokenness. It identified him to all who saw him as a beggar. He was seen by society as a man that would never amount to anything. There were some who had pity on him and would give him a few coins, but on this day he was seen as an irritant who needed to be quieted and brushed aside. You are not defined by what you have done, nor by

> You are not defined by what you have done, nor by the defects in your humanity.

the defects in your humanity. You are given the liberty to take off that cloak of brokenness. When you come to the Master, you do not have to be identified by your past actions – again, you are not what you have done. As you seek forgiveness from God and ask for restoration, accept the mercy and grace He bestows upon you, and then continue to follow Him.

The second step toward forgiving yourself is confessing all your sins. Every time I lead a person to Christ and pray for salvation in their lives, it always includes asking God to forgive them, to remove all past sins and actions that were contrary to what God requires of us. I then tell them to confess their sins to God while I am praying for them. The Scriptures tell us, *"If we confess our sins, he is faithful and just to forgive us our sins, and to cleanse us from all unrighteousness."*[105] In order for God to restore you, He must first remove all that has tarnished your life.

As you confess your failures, sins, mistakes, lustful thoughts, and errors in your past, God cleanses you and makes you a new creature in His sight. This confession is between you and God, and is something you can do right now in a private place. You can be sitting in your car, your bedroom, or in a private jail cell – as far as God is concerned it really does not matter. He is just waiting for you, so that He can cleanse you and make you new. If you haven't done it before or it's been a long time since you have confessed your sins to God, go ahead and put this book down right now and start praying.

> My prayer for you is that your heart is truly open to receive...

My prayer for you is that your heart is truly open to receive the release God has for you as you unburden all the vices that have kept you away from Him.

The final step toward forgiving yourself is receiving the love and forgiveness of God. **God's love is unconditional.** You don't have to pay Him for His love. God wants a relationship with you and Scripture makes this clear. Jesus offers us rest from our burdens if we will only come to Him: *"Come unto me, all ye that labour and are heavy laden, and I will give you rest."*[106] Sometimes, it's hard to believe God will forgive us regardless of what we have done wrong, but He does! In this final step toward forgiving yourself, I want you to grasp the revelation that just because you don't feel forgiven, does not mean you are not forgiven. **Do not base God's Word and His promises on your feelings – feelings can never match up to or supersede the Word of God.** Jesus Himself stated, *"Heaven and earth shall pass away, but my words shall not pass away."*[107] Another great Scripture makes it very clear that when we start following Christ and living a Christian life, sin no longer has a hold over us, no matter how we feel:

*"But if we walk in the light, as he is in the light, we have fellowship one with another, and the blood of Jesus Christ his Son cleanseth us from all sin." – 1 John 1:7 (KJV)*

Do your best always to remember that feelings are no more than an emotional barometer of how you perceive your situation, but God's Word reminds us that when we are in Christ, *"we walk by faith, not by sight."*[108] Which means your faith in God and His Word are always superior to how you might feel. When doubt enters your mind, here is another good passage to remember:

*"If we confess our sins, he is faithful and just to forgive us our sins, and to cleanse us from all unrighteousness." – 1 John 1:9 (KJV)*

Read this Scripture out loud to confirm your new or renewed relationship with Christ, which qualifies you to receive all His promises. Declare God's Word when you pray, using Scriptures like those above to remind yourself – and any other force which may come against you – that your sins are no longer held against you. As a child of God and a joint heir of Christ,[109] remember that, *"greater is he that is in you, than he that is in the world."*[110]

As you reflect upon God's grace in your life, you can begin the process of forgiving yourself by actively claiming and believing the promises contained in God's Word. The enemy will keep reminding you of your defeat. He will point to your past, your brokenness, and flaunt it before

> " **The enemy will keep reminding you of your defeat.**

you. Satan knows that if you pick up the mantle of God's Word and begin to swing it, he will be in serious trouble concerning his attempts to control your life. He does not want you to believe the promises of God. He wants you to focus on your guilt. The devil reminds me of a boxer who speaks a lot of 'smack' before a fight. He says all kinds of nonsense that doesn't make any sense – he does so just to confuse and confound his contender.

As a kid, I loved watching boxing matches, but I was more enthralled with what was said by the boxers outside the ring before any fight. Muhammad Ali was the best in talking smack! He once said:

*"I done wrestled with an alligator, I done tussled with a whale; handcuffed lightning, thrown thunder in jail; only last week, I murdered a rock, injured a stone, hospitalized a brick; I'm so mean I make medicine sick!"*[111]

Impossible, crazy, but he spoke fear into many men before he even entered the ring. He knew that if he could win the mind game, he would win the fight. The moment you begin believing all the negative statements that have been said about you, you've lost. When you believe

> The moment you begin believing all the negative statements that have been said...

you can't pick up the pieces, you never will. Again, Muhammad Ali hit the nail on the head with this powerful and very true quotation: *"Inside of a ring or out, aint nothing wrong with going down. It's staying down that's wrong."*[112]

**FORGIVE YOURSELF**

Forgiving yourself starts in your own mind. It really is a mind game. What you accept as fact will remain a fact and what you accept as fiction or frivolous will remain as such. What you have to do is make sure you have the facts clear and all your ducks lined up in the right row.

**ACCEPTING THAT WHICH IS TRUE**

You need to accept the truth! This includes the fact that you have experienced failure, and this failure has affected your life, as well as those around you. It is a useful exercise to list some of these basic truths:

- I messed up. I failed. I made a terrible mistake.
- I was responsible for every decision I made that brought me to this place.
- My actions hurt people I love – emotionally, physically, financially, and spiritually.
- My actions brought shame on me as well as those close to me.

**REFUSING TO ACCEPT THAT WHICH IS UNTRUE**

These are things people have said about you concerning your character which label you in a way that defines you unfairly, especially due to the perpetual nature of the accusations. You may have fitted the label attached to these sins for a moment in time, but this label need not define

> ...but this label need not define who you are for the rest of your life.

who you are for the rest of your life. These labels include accusations such as: he is a liar; he is a thief; he is a pervert; he is an adulterer; he is a philanderer; etcetera. These terms label you in perpetuity, even though we are freed from labels when we enter into a personal relationship with Jesus Christ, as He cleanses *"us from all unrighteousness."*[113] You may even have said some of the following statements to yourself or allowed them to keep drifting around in your mind:

- I am no good to anyone anymore.
- I can never be trusted again.
- I should never be given another chance.
- I'm a drunk, a drug addict, an adulterer, and that can never change.

- My family and friends would be better off if I just ended it all.

You can fill in the blanks in either category. I'm sure those who are brutally honest would probably add even more self-depreciating statements to the list above. But what is most important is to measure each statement against the Word of God. Too often, in the category

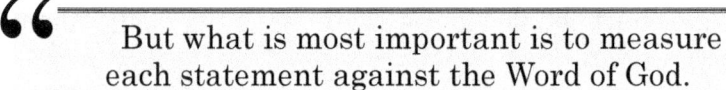

> But what is most important is to measure each statement against the Word of God.

reflecting basic truths, we have added all the untruths. In the minds of most people there is only one category. You can never forgive yourself if you hold onto these untruths. Take courage from the fact that you have finally reached this point of self-discovery. You have reached this point because you've taken responsibility, and you earnestly want to pick up the pieces and move on with your life. There may be just a tiny glimmer of hope within you which allows you to think, against all odds, that maybe it is possible for you to pick up the pieces and see your life being restored in some positive fashion. And you would be correct in thinking that, for this is a gospel truth!

Your failure places you in a position where God can move in your life. Don't let the mind games of the enemy defeat you without you even trying to climb back into the ring of life. Sure, you'll take a few licks, perhaps even be knocked down again, but it's in standing to your feet once more that you will be made stronger. **There are truths and untruths – be sure to discern what is true and what is false.** With Christ, all things are possible. Therefore, anything that speaks contrary to this can be chalked up to an untruth and discarded.

Here is an exercise for you to complete. Sit down with a blank sheet of paper and at the top of the page, write down your failure. Following that, create a list, writing down each step of the process you are conscious of that brought you to this place of failure. Be honest and don't blame others – this is about you and for your own benefit. Next, write down each thing people have said about you as a result of your failure. Finally, write down all the things you have thought about yourself since you messed up.

Take a moment now to consider the grace, mercy and strength God is bringing into your life. Now, put a line through each item that does not match up with this statement: I am more than a conqueror through Him that loves me.[114]

What is left will represent the facts. They are neutral and not accusatory. They represent the real issues that brought you to a place of brokenness; nothing more, nothing less. When you review everything you crossed off, you will find each statement was negative in nature. It was either self-destructive in its purpose if constructed by your own mind, or it contradicts Scripture if constructed by other people.

Both these aspects of a negative belief system are contrary to the truth that we are newborn creatures in Christ once we have accepted Jesus as Lord and Savior:

*"Therefore if any man be in Christ, he is a new creature: old things are passed away; behold, all things are become new." – 2 Corinthians 5:17 (KJV)*

You might be thinking that you actually had already accepted Christ into your life as Lord and Savior before experiencing the failure that has crippled your progress. Don't allow this to thwart you from humbling yourself in repentance, for God favors a contrite heart. Jesus personally experienced temptation, so He understands the potential for human failure. That is why God built a failsafe mechanism into His redemption plan for humanity through Jesus:

*"If we confess our sins, he is faithful and just to forgive us our sins, and*

*to cleanse us from all unrighteousness." – 1 John 1:9 (KJV)*

> Failure does not have to be permanent!

We have no excuse. Failure does not have to be permanent! Now, go ahead and burn that piece of paper. Every time the enemy whispers one of those untruths into your ear or someone tries to label you with a past failing, remember that you erased these untruths by burning them in the fire. They no longer have any sway over your life, and neither do they have any strength against you. Win this mind game and you are well on your way to picking up the pieces and living a victorious and restored life in Christ.

**FORGIVING OTHERS**

Irrespective of how others choose to act, it is incumbent upon you to take the time to forgive those who have hurt you. There might be a list of individuals who need your forgiveness. This list may include the person you partnered with who helped you create the mess you find yourself in; the individual who informed the authorities – or your boss or your spouse, depending on the context of your failure; the people who had nothing nice to say about you; others who exaggerated the story, adding untruths about what happened; those who you thought were friends who took the initiative in leading the charge against you. **The hurt, disappointment, and anger can come in any form and through various actions, but the reality of these emotions cannot be denied.** Only your faith in Christ can dispel these feelings and heal you of any bitterness.

I attempt to live my renewed life in this manner: I treat others in the way I wish to be treated. If I want to be blessed, I need to first bless others. A couple years after my failure, I read a newspaper article about another minister who was going to court for charges of immorality. I knew who he was and drove the several hours to where he lived to let him know that I was praying for him. Regardless of his innocence or guilt, I was not there to judge, but to pray and bring some genuine comfort into his life. I was treating another the way I wanted to be treated. So, if I want

> **"** If I am seeking forgiveness, then I first need to forgive others.

a second chance, then I first need to be willing to give others another chance. If I am seeking forgiveness, then I first need to forgive others . In fact, Jesus specifically requires us to forgive others. Scripture makes this very clear:

*"For if ye forgive men their trespasses, your heavenly Father will also forgive you: 15 But if ye forgive not men their trespasses, neither will your Father forgive your trespasses." – Matthew 6:14-15 (KJV)*

A predicament occasionally experienced as a result of failure is the manner in which we must choose to deal with those who refuse to accept our apology... those who continue in their quest to make life as difficult as possible or who continue to gossip about our failure. Do not let their actions dictate a reaction from you. Rather respond with the love of Christ wherever possible, and do not allow their lack of mercy to embitter your life. Since experiencing God's power to restore my life, I still have had to endure some difficult times. My wife and I would occasionally attend a certain function or event where we would encounter people who were aware of my past failure. When these people, even those in leadership, became aware of our presence, they would respond by being rude to us, or would allow their bitterness towards me to be clearly reflected for others to see. There would be times after leaving an event that my wife would begin to cry… and I knew this was all due to my past failure. I would become angry, because even after so many years, these people believed they had the right to remind me of my past. In fact, they treated it almost as if it were their right and obligation to stand in judgment against me for my past failure. I would take my wife's hand, reminding both her and myself that we need to pray for those who struggle with forgiveness. I would go on to remind my wife that we were fully committed to preventing their judgmental spirits from planting seeds of bitterness within us – **for our God truly is greater than anything that comes against us!** Even so, I just hate the fact that my wife has had to endure such public ridicule! Yet, I must stress once more how very thankful I am for her unconditional love and resolve, even when it hurts. So, just remember to extend to others the forgiveness you seek.

You cannot find forgiveness until you take the time to forgive yourself. When you have learned to forgive yourself using the steps outlined in this chapter, you will find your posture improved, with your shoulders no longer drooping in an attitude of dejection. You will be able to look people in the eye again, and you will feel like you are on a more solid footing as you pick up the pieces and move into your future.

*Your Thoughts...*

# Chapter Eight
## Rejection is God's Protection[115]

*"God does not remove us from all harm;
He uses harm to move us close to Him"*
- **Dillon Burroughs**

There is not a single human being on the earth who has not felt rejected at one time or another. It's the nature of the fallen world in which we live. When everything is taken into consideration, most people will default to doing what is best

> Rejection can sting!

for them at the expense of another. Rejection can sting! It leaves us with feelings of self-doubt, insecurity and anger. Don't get me wrong – it's always good to take self-inventory of your emotional health, but I want to give you a new perspective on rejection. The truth is that I was looking for things in other people that only God could give and had already given me. The reason being rejected is so painful is because we have put some kind of expectation on that person that they were never intended to meet.

### DOES REJECTION DIMINISH OUR WORTH?

Rejection is certain to occur when we value people's opinion of us above God's. When people close to us reject us, Satan quickly plants seeds of rebellion (why should I respect them or love them if they don't accept or respect me?), bitterness, and guilt, which result in an intentional or

>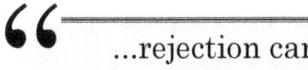
> ...rejection can make us think we are of less importance, or undeserving...

subconscious avoidance of people, and certain situations. Feelings of rejection can make us think we are of less importance, or undeserving, and that other people's acceptance would mean approval. This can lead us to strain towards being something or someone else, other than who God made us to be. We must reject the Deceivers lies.

Because my own sense of self-worth, my perceived value, is bound to my work as a pastor and minister of the Gospel, studying and teaching the Word, the rejection of people would have a negative effect on my feeling of self-worth. Where do you find your worth? If it were taken from you, how would you feel? In some cultures men find their masculinity and worth by climbing a ninety-foot tower and jumping off this tower with only an eighty-foot vine attached to their ankle.

In another, women perceive their worth according to the length of their necks. They take rings of copper tubing, placing them around their neck to push their shoulders down and their head up. Every six months, more copper tubing is added, progressively stretching the neck to ever longer lengths. In yet another culture, value is perceived by how much individuals can stretch their earlobes, to the extent where you could pass a softball through them. Many western cultures perceive value as having a fit and toned body with flat abdominal muscles.

How do we measure our success and worth? **We must learn to see ourselves as God sees us and not how people see or define us**. The people who have rejected you are not tied to your destiny. They do not define who you are or what you are. Our value is not found in who we are, but whose we are. Did Jesus sit around asking, "Why don't they like me?" No. He was about the Father's business, and in doing so, He walked in the knowledge that He was a Son, fully accepted and secure in His Father's provision:

*"Jesus saith unto them Did ye never read the scriptures, The stone which the builders rejected, the same is become the head of the corner: this is the Lord's doing, and it is marvellous in our eyes?" – Matthew 21:42 (KJV)*

**What if people's rejection was really God's protection?**

What if rejection by someone else is God's way of protecting you while you mature in the truth of what He has been saying to you all along? Whatever the situation is that you're in – who you are or what you may have done – it really doesn't make a difference when it comes to rejection. It's going to happen. It's just a matter of what you are going to choose to believe in that particular situation. Your feelings of rejection don't change the truth of what God says about you, and who He says you are. You must keep in mind that Jesus, the author of creation, knew what it felt like to be rejected by His own people and even His own disciples. The fact of the matter is, when you look at it Scripturally, God's perfect plan came to fruition because of the rejections Jesus encountered. David, in Psalm 139, tells us that our score is determined by how God ranks us – not people:

*"Search me, O God, and know my heart: try me, and know my thoughts: 24 And see if there be any wicked way in me, and lead me in the way everlasting." – Psalm 139:23-24 (KJV)*

David recognized that God knew everything he had done, right and

> He knew that God had a plan for his life, regardless of his mistakes.

wrong, and yet God still loved him. He knew that God had a plan for his life, regardless of his mistakes.

If we trust God *"that all things work together for good to them that love God, to them who are the called according to his purpose,"*[116] then rejection can be used by God in the plan He has for our lives. Joseph was rejected and was sold into slavery by his brothers, who were jealous of him and saw him as a dreamer.[117] God used this to later save their family and the nation of Israel.

Moses killed an Egyptian to help his fellow Jews and they rejected him for it.[118] God used him to lead the nation of Israel out of bondage and into the Promised Land. Leah was rejected[119] by Jacob for her more attractive sister, Rachel, but God sent Jesus, the world's Saviour, through the line of Judah,[120] one of Leah's sons.[121]

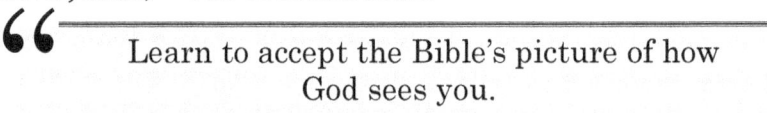

> Learn to accept the Bible's picture of how God sees you.

Learn to accept the Bible's picture of how God sees you. You are part of God's royal family; a child of our heavenly King, heir to the throne of life.[122] Everything the Father has will one day be yours. This cannot change due to anything any person ever says to you. The fear of rejection can make us defensive, causing us to erect a wall around ourselves which reads something into every word or action of others, and creates a hardness which robs us of our compassion.

I read about a young lady who had been mentored for the past couple of years. The minister who had been her mentor was impressed at her progress. She had come a long way! When he first heard about her, she was a total wreck! She was losing faith in God. He remembered her saying that she wasn't even sure if there was a God. Like most of us, she was having her share of trials and tribulations and was ready to give up. For years she and her fiancé had been trying to purchase a home and start a family, but it seemed like every time they made one step, something would push them back two steps! After being with her boyfriend of three years, he decided a week before their wedding day that she wasn't "the one" for him. During the latest conversation with her mentor, she was all smiles as she shared the news that she had just purchased her first home. She said, "I thank God for my unanswered

> " I thank God for my unanswered prayers.

prayers." They both shared a laugh because that was actually something he would always say to her, and she would always frown and shake her head in disbelief. She went on to say that now it was all very clear to her. Every setback and roadblock had been for her good. She explained that if she had had her way, she would probably be going through a divorce right now, stuck with a house she no longer wanted... she even feared the possibility that she may have become a single parent had her prayers been answered. God knew what she didn't know, and sometimes rejection is God's protection!

**ONLY IN GOD CAN PEACE AND SECURITY BE FOUND.**

Identity in Christ says you are perfect, spotless and blameless. You are not going to hear that truth anywhere other than from the Holy Spirit and God's Word: *"For he hath made him to be sin for us, who knew no sin; that we might be made the righteousness of God in him."*[123]

**We constantly look for other people to validate us.** We put this constant subconscious pressure and expectation on them, which they can never meet, while all the time God is saying to born-again believers "You are my child in whom I am well pleased."

God gives you security in Jesus. True, peace-giving security comes only from Jesus:

*"Peace I leave with you, my peace I give unto you: not as the world giveth, give I unto you. Let not your heart be troubled, neither let it be afraid."*[124] Christians are storm-proofed, not storm-free in this life, so if

> " Christians are storm-proofed, not storm-free in this life...

your security does not come from knowing Jesus, then you will constantly deal with disappointment and rejection.

Only Jesus gives the unconditional acceptance we often snub in favor of the approval of others. People inherently want to feel accepted by others, and I understand that. However, there is only One in the universe who makes the claim, *"I will never leave you nor forsake you"*: *"Let your conversation be without covetousness; and be content with such things as ye have: for he hath said, I will never leave thee, nor forsake thee."*[125]

In Jill Morgan's book, A Man of The Word – The Life of G Campbell Morgan,[126] she quotes part of the story about a man considered to be one of the greatest evangelists of modern history, G. Campbell Morgan. In 1888, he stood before three men who had the power to determine, "Is he called to preach, or is he not called to preach?" Morgan stood with other young, hopeful preachers, and they all preached for these three men, and at the end of the day, these three men posted an "accepted" and "rejected" list. G. Campbell Morgan went and looked for his name on the accepted list, and it was not there. He was crushed. He looked on the second list, and there his name was as one who was rejected. Devastated, he sent his dad a telegram, and he simply wrote one word on the telegram: rejected. A few days later though, his very wise dad sent a telegram back, and G. Campbell Morgan said that message from his father changed his life forever. The telegram simply said, "Rejected by men, accepted in Heaven." After he wired to his father the one word, "Rejected," he sat down to write in his diary: "Very dark everything seems. Still, He knoweth best." Many years later, as he looked back across the years, he said, "I thank God to-day, for closing that door of hope, because, when He turned my feet in another direction I found the breadth of His commandments, and the glory of His service."[127]

**FORGIVENESS**

Rejection can cut us deeply, but with rejection must come forgiveness. As fast as you rush to disinfect a cut on your hand, so must you rush to follow the instruction of God[128] to forgive. Jesus gave us two commandments, to love God and to love each other.[129] Love is the exact

> Love is the exact opposite of unforgivingness, pride and bitterness.

opposite of unforgivingness, pride and bitterness. You can't truly love somebody and hold bitterness or unforgivingness against him or her simultaneously. It is our responsibility to forgive others. God sent His Son Jesus to die for our sins, so that we may be reconciled to Him, without spot or blemish. He asks that we give others the same forgiveness that paid for us. In the parable of the unforgiving servant,[130] the king says:

*"O thou wicked servant, I forgave thee all that debt, because thou desiredst me: 33 Shouldest not thou also have had compassion on thy fellowservant, even as I had pity on thee? 34 And his lord was wroth, and delivered him to the tormentors, till he should pay all that was due unto him. 35 So likewise shall my heavenly Father do also unto you, if ye from your hearts forgive not every one his brother their trespasses." – Matthew 18:32-35 (KJV)*

This is echoed in Matthew 6:15, "But if ye forgive not men their trespasses, neither will your Father forgive your trespasses." Often what seems to be an unanswered prayer could be a "no," or a "not yet" from God for our protection, as He knows what is best for us. But, when we pray with unforgivingness in our hearts, we could be blocking our prayers from being answered: *"And when ye stand praying, forgive, if ye have ought against any: that your Father also which is in heaven may forgive you your trespasses."*[131] So when we abide in the vine which is Jesus, and forgive others who have rejected us, it opens us up to God's forgiveness,[132] it puts us in a receiving position when we pray,[133] it helps us become spiritually fruitful,[134] and we will know that we have passed from spiritual death to being reconciled with our heavenly Father when we love each other.[135] When we keep God's commandments and love and

> When we keep God's commandments and love and forgive one another…

forgive one another, we prove that we love Jesus ,[136] and we abide in Christ's love![137] What a magnificent blessing forgiveness really is!

Rejection by other human beings carries with it an extremely debilitating emotion. Some emotions, like those attached to rejection, are often difficult to process, especially if the individual has no prior experience in dealing with these emotions. The spiritual exercises below offer some basic steps with practical applications that will help put an individual on the path to processing rejection and the destructive emotion it subsequently elicits. As with the entire process of restoration, acknowledging the emotion attached to rejection is a necessary step.

## *Spiritual Exercises*

### 1.) **DON'T DENY YOUR FEELINGS**

Do not deny any of your feelings, it is so important to actually feel your initial feelings, acknowledge them and release them. This could mean going out for a run, jumping on a trampoline or writing. However you do this, you want to make sure you acknowledge and feel your feelings that come up first and then release them to God.

### 2. SHIFT (RENEW) YOUR THOUGHTS[138]

*"And be not conformed to this world: but be ye transformed by the renewing of your mind, that ye may prove what is that good, and acceptable, and perfect, will of God."*[139] Thoughts are powerful and have an effect on your feelings and your behavior – "For as he thinketh in his heart, so is he:..."[140] Once you have released the emotions caused by the rejection, change your thoughts to focus on God's unconditional love and acceptance.

### 3. TRUST & BELIEVE

Trust God that His Word is true and consider the mighty plans He has for you: *"For I know the thoughts that I think toward you, saith the Lord, thoughts of peace, and not of evil, to give you (hope in*[141]*) an expected end."*[142] Lloyd Ogilvie,[143] the distinguished Presbyterian minister who served as Chaplain of the United States Senate from the 104th through 107th Congresses (1995- 2003), made this his motto:

*"Secure in God's love, I will not surrender my self-worth to the opinions and judgments of others. When I am rejected, I will not retaliate. When I am hurt, I will allow God's love to heal me, and knowing the pain of rejection, I will seek to love those who suffer from its anguish."*[144]

In the first line he says Secure in God's love, I will not surrender my self-

He chose to please God over pleasing man.

worth to the opinions and the judgments of others. He chose to please God over pleasing man. He then acknowledges the "when" of the hurt. It will come, but he puts his trust in God to heal such hurts. And finally, because he can relate to such hurts, he is committed to being the ointment of love for those who are suffering from such hurt.

**FEAR OF REJECTION**

The logical response to the pain of rejection is to avoid any situation where it may recur. Like the fear of failure, which paralyzes us from moving forward in our ministry or our walk with God, the fear of rejection instills in us a false sense of self-worth. The fear of rejection is ultimately an anxiety concerning how others feel about us. God's Word

> The fear of rejection is ultimately an anxiety concerning how others feel about us.

says *"The fear of man bringeth a snare: but whoso putteth his trust in the Lord shall be safe."*[145] The fear of rejection is really a fear of man, a noose or trap that binds us in an apprehension of any relationships. Jesus' great commission to us is to make disciples,[146] and discipleship is relationship,[147] so this is also a tactic of the enemy to prevent the spread of God's redemptive plan of salvation. Perhaps it is time to practice some rejection of our own – rejection of the fear of failure and rejection. Only if we place God first in our lives can we live free of the fear of failure and rejection in our lives, because God has not given us the spirit of fear, but of power, and of love, and of a sound mind.[148]

*"Be still and know that I am God."*[149] Elijah became fearful and discouraged, and felt the sting of rejection after it became obvious that there would be no immediate revival in the land, even after the people had witnessed the fire from heaven consume the sacrifice.[150] This great man of God deserted his post and ran for his life. While he hid in a cave at

Horeb, God spoke to him... not in the rock shattering wind, the dreadful earthquake, nor the sudden fire that followed, but in a gentle blowing, in that of a faint whisper.[151] When you are rejected, don't go to God with a description of your pain and humiliation, He knows because He has experienced it many times. Be still before Him and allow Him to comfort you and to strengthen you. Do as David counseled himself, *"My soul, wait thou only upon God, for my expectation is from Him. He only is my rock and my salvation, He is my defence; I shall not be moved."*[152] Part of Elijah's problem lay in his expectations. The fulfillment of our expectations must

> The fulfillment of our expectations must never be the source of our happiness...

never be the source of our happiness, neither must our expectations become our confidence in God. We must learn to rest our expectations in God's sovereignty.[153]

The next time your feelings of rejection surface, go before God and ask Him to reveal His truths to you. "Father, am I your beloved child? Holy Spirit, am I safe and secure in Your hands? Jesus, do you accept me unconditionally?" Then quietly wait for the Holy Spirit. If you are not hearing an unmistakable "yes" to those questions, then you're not hearing from God, because His Word answers all those questions with a "yes" and without reproach. So be aware that people's rejection can be your heavenly Father's protection.

# Chapter Nine
## Rebuilding Your Credibility[154]

*"The more you are willing to accept responsibility for your actions, the more credibility you will have."*
– **Brian Koslow**[155]

Can you be trusted again? Should you be given another chance? Someone who knows you and who is aware of your failure is probably asking these questions. The amazing thing about relationships is that when an individual believes (has confidence) in another, a bond is developed which includes trust, care, and concern. To answer the question: **"Can I rebuild my credibility?"** – the answer is, "Yes!" What must be understood at the outset is that the reconstruction of your credibility involves a detailed process – it will never be just a quick-fix, one-day project. Rebuilding your trustworthiness requires a developed plan of action, honesty, vulnerability, and time.

> " Rebuilding your trustworthiness requires a developed plan of action...

When you utilize and work with all of these ingredients, the end result will be a "new you."

The Bible gives us a powerful promise of being able to start over. The Apostle Paul, addressing the church in Corinth, expressed this truth very clearly: *"Therefore if any man be in Christ, he is a new creature: old things are passed away; behold, all things are become new."*[156] This is the first phase of your action plan. You must involve God. He must be your foundation and at the center of all you do. Remember, God did not bring you to this failed state you find yourself in. He is, however, attempting to draw you toward Him to create something new or renewed within you.

Several years ago, I was invited to speak before a special assembly at the United Nations. In my delivery, I spoke about the wonderful vision this entity had developed. I also addressed their Millennium Development Goals (MDGs).[157] These range from reducing by half the extreme global poverty we currently face, to stopping the spread of HIV/AIDS, and even developing a universal primary education. I expressed how these goals were all wonderful and commendable. In my final comments, I addressed the struggles experienced by the UN organization, and pointed out the plain fact that in all they do, God is not consulted nor involved in any of the processes they implement. I emphasized a simple matter of fact: the UN has no place for God within the structure of their organization. In an attempt to highlight an evident shortfall in their current methodology, I mentioned that if they did not put God at the center of their work, they would never reach their goals. I closed my address by quoting from the

>  I mentioned that if they did not put God at the center…

Book of the Chronicles:

*"If my people, which are called by my name, shall humble themselves, and pray, and seek my face, and turn from their wicked ways; then will I hear from heaven, and will forgive their sin, and will heal their land." – 2 Chronicles 7:14 (KJV)*

My personal journey started by believing in the God of the Bible. A relationship with Jesus Christ is the major prerequisite to this door of new beginnings being opened. This may be a matter of simple acceptance for some, while for others it may seem like a far stretch. I understand both mindsets, for I have experienced both positions. I share with you my personal testimony along with what I have witnessed during my years in ministry. I can attest to seeing how God has moved in the lives of so many people, creating a positive effect which cannot be denied. God truly is real and He transforms the lives of those who accept Him. As you choose to start this journey or begin anew, and develop a relationship with God, I promise that not too far down the road, you will know that God is real.

What drew me into His presence was my hunger for something unknown, and a feeling of emptiness I couldn't explain. It was more then twenty six years ago that I first realized the truth of God's existence, yet I remember it just as if it were yesterday. God spoke to me in a very personal way for the first time through a sermon being delivered by a pastor. I was shocked and amazed at the same time. I remember formulating specific questions in my mind while the sermon was being delivered, and as each question took shape in my mind, an answer was directly presented to me through the spoken Word of God's messenger. Life's journey brought me to that moment in place and time, just as God has drawn you to this unique moment in time so He can speak into your life though these words.

> Life's journey brought me to that moment in place and time...

You will find it is through Christ that your credibility will be rebuilt. As He begins to stir your heart and work in you, you will find yourself changing from within. Your attitudes and thoughts will be reshaped and re-designed by the Master Himself. Bad experiences with Christians, people in positions of leadership, and other people who have adversely affected you should not be used as a reason to blame God and keep your distance from Him. Remember, these people are just as imperfect as you. The beauty of God's grace is that you have the right and the blessing to go to the Master directly. Once you have connected or reconnected with Christ, you can move onto phase two of your action plan.

> ❝ ...God's grace is that you have the right and the blessing to go to the Master directly.

In phase two, you must bring accountability into your life. I have often heard parents tell their children what they expect from them. They shout instructions at the children then scold them when they disobey. Yet these same parents do not demonstrate willful obedience to authority within their own lives. This behavior reinforces a confusing and contradictory message to the children: "Do as I say, not as I do!" **When gauging our integrity, people generally judge us by our actions rather than our words.**

Speaking the correct words in an attempt to redress failure can be an important first step, but words to this effect are useless if not followed by appropriate action. For this reason we need to stop and take ownership of our failures when we make mistakes. You either did or did not do what you were supposed to, but regardless of your failing, you must own it! An important distinction that I cannot re-emphasize enough is that you do not become what you own. I own two little dogs, but that does not make me a dog! Therefore, do not label yourself with your failure.

When you own something, you are responsible for it. **You are in charge of your own destiny in Christ**, and with that ownership you can decide how to extract the most benefit from both your failures and your successes. This formula served me well in my own failing: I failed and therefore, since I own that failure, I needed to *address* it; I had to go through whatever process was required of me to redress the *consequences* of my actions; I had to *make it right* whenever there was a possibility; I needed to *learn* how to not do it again: and then I was required to *move forward.*

To *address* something means to think about and deal with the issue or problem at hand.[158] This means I take full responsibility for the actions that brought me to this place. I no longer blame it on someone else or claim that it is the result of my environment. I did it!

## THE CONSEQUENCES

Whatever the fallout, a concerted effort must be made to redress the negative repercussions of your failure, and the actions that need to be taken must be adhered too. It may seem unacceptable, unfair, or perhaps considered even worse than the action that landed you in this predicament. But remember, the point is rebuilding your credibility. Therefore, as my father would say to me, "Suck it up!" Remember, you want to reach the place were you have regained trust and have been restored, in some fashion. The actions which led to your failure have stripped away your right to demand something else for your punishment.

> " Remember, you want to reach the place were you have regained trust...

## MAKE IT RIGHT

You cannot go back and undo what has been done. But you can take every step within your means to correct as much as you can. Tell that individual you are sorry and then back it up by action. Ask them what you can do in an attempt to make it right. This is what I did. I remember sitting there and asking, "What can I do?" I then went ahead and did what was asked. In the back of my mind, I considered that what was being asked may have been too much, but in my spirit I was immediately reminded that this was the cost of doing business with sin. **You need to know in your heart and mind when you look back that you did or are doing all you can.** How others act or react during or after you complete this task should have no bearing on your own actions.

### LEARN FROM IT

Look at what you did wrong and put into place the safe guards that will keep you from going down that road again. This is to ensure that you are not labeled a "repeat offender" by others. This may mean changing your friends. If hanging with them brings trouble into your life, they should no longer be your friends. Of course, you should try to introduce them to Christ first, but if they choose not to have a relationship with Jesus, then the effort involved in maintaining such a friendship will most likely outweigh the benefit you receive from their friendship. If handling money is too tempting, then steer clear of these situations and do not accept invitations to handle money. Just as a surgeon is called in to cut out a tumor to restore the health of an individual, so must you cut those things out of your life that will lead to self-destruction.

### MOVE FORWARD

Treat every day as a fresh, blank canvas. Do not keep looking back – lingering in the past will prevent you from living in the present! Rather look forward to the possibilities and blessings you are receiving. Become the brush and allow God to be the artist. Watch as He uses you to paint a beautiful picture of promise on the canvas of your life. As you focus on today, remember to keep God at the center of your life. The Apostle Peter learned this when he was on the boat in a storm. Remember, as

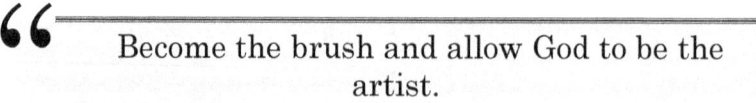

> Become the brush and allow God to be the artist.

that boat was being tossed around in the sea, all the disciples saw Jesus walking on the sea. When Peter saw Jesus, he asked if it really was Him, and if so, if He would call out to Peter to come to Him. So Jesus called to Peter to come. Peter stepped out of the boat and began to walk on water. However, the winds were boisterous, and when Peter looked at the waves he became afraid and began to sink.[159] As soon as Peter took his eyes off the Lord and focused on what was happening around him, he put himself in jeopardy. As you move forward, keep focused on the Word

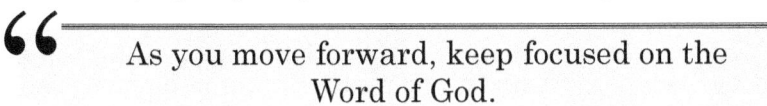

> As you move forward, keep focused on the Word of God.

of God. Spend time each day reading His Word. Spend time in meditation, sharing your thoughts, fears, and desires with Him. Throughout the day, in every decision you make, reflect upon whether God would bless or rebuke such an action or attitude, and strive to live according to His will and not your own.

Intertwined within these actions are two additional ingredients essential to you rising above your failure: honesty and vulnerability. These elements must be molded into your character and mixed into everything you do. Bread will never rise without added yeast! Similarly, without adding honesty and vulnerability to your character, you are at risk of never rising above failure to attain the integrity God desires His children to incorporate into their lives. Addressing criticisms from a neutral emotional state of mind allows you to deal with criticism in the moment the experience is unfolding. You can enforce boundaries placed in your spirit by God that protects you, but at the same time, does not have you pre-emptively striking out at others from your unfounded fears. When criticism happens as the result of another person venting in an improper way, you can withdraw from such engagement that could possibly result in more harm than good.

Where honesty is concerned, it is essential to first be honest with yourself. We can convince ourselves of anything if we want to, but that does not mean it is right. Through the process of being responsible, every step you take must be an honest one. What you say and what you do must be honest. This means it has to be real and true, with no ulterior motive to justify yourself or your actions – honesty is all-inclusive. You cannot just tell a half-truth, it must be all the truth. This is the only way you will ever regain trust.

> "We can convince ourselves of anything if we want to, but that doesn't mean it is right.

Another aspect of honesty is a commitment to being forthright. The omission of certain facts or the specific history of an event in question is not a bypass for honesty. A difficult issue some people may have to deal with is the ability to leave the past in the past while working in the present, and yet being conscious that any omission of the past does not sabotage their road to restoration. A case in point is a meeting I once had with a few people of whom one was an influential individual. We talked on several occasions, and they finally requested a meeting with me to discuss the potential of partnering on future efforts. I was very excited as we discussed concepts and strategies.

We concluded the meeting and were moving into the next phase when a question came up. I immediately realized I needed to share with them this past failure in my life, to make sure it did not have an impact on what we would do together. When we met again I shared this information. They were disappointed that I did not bring this up in our previous meeting. When asked why I did not, I explained that I had not given it a thought because it was in my past. I tried to make them understand that when I thought about my failure, it always stirred up painful emotions related to this dark period in my life, which I simply chose to lock away so as not to think about it any more. They understood, but felt I should have been as transparent as they had been. The result was a strain on our relationship for a period of time. It was a setback in building my credibility with them, but it did not end the relationship.

You do not have to wear your failure on your sleeve, nor shout it out for all the world to know. However, you must always consider the new people who come into your life, and how your future dealings with them may be affected if you omit to inform them of a significant failure in your life. If your failure might have a negative effect on others, or hurt a relationship, you must be transparent and forthright from the outset.

> " You do not have to wear your failure on your sleeve...

If, as a result of being forthright you lose that relationship or opportunity, you will still have your integrity intact, which is always more important in the long run. Another door will open or that door which closed may reopen at a later date. Regardless of what happens, just remember, complete honesty will prevent you from ever having to ask yourself the question: "What if they find out?"

This issue of omission is where vulnerability can really be felt. **When you make yourself vulnerable, you open yourself up to be judged, hurt, and rejected.** No one likes any of these things to happen. When you honestly repent and it is not received, it hurts. When you've changed your ways and you are still judged negatively for your past, it seems unfair. When people blatantly reject and ignore you, it invariably brings about a horrible, sinking feeling in your gut. I've experienced the devastating feeling of rejection, and it can easily bring about a depressed state of mind, especially when you are working so hard to do the right thing and to walk in integrity.

I was a passenger on an overseas flight, scheduled to change planes before reaching my final destination. While I was sitting in my seat reading, people were boarding the plane. At some point I happened to look up just as one particular individual walked down the aisle. Our eyes locked for a split second before I lowered mine back to the book I was reading. While getting back into my book, I thought to myself that I had seen a hint of recognition in that passenger's eyes. As my mind considered a possible connection, it dawned on me – I knew this man and he definitely knew me. When we landed, I deplaned before him and stood in the seating area waiting for him to disembark. As he walked into the seating area, he looked directly at me with utter disdain. I turned and went my way. In that moment I realized some people will judge you, condemn you, or hold your failure against you no matter what you do to redeem the situation, or how earnestly you seek restoration. You simply have to learn that this unabated judgment of you is their issue and not yours.

I opened this chapter by asking you two questions: Can you be trusted again? Should you be given another chance? The answer to both will always depend on you and who you are asking. Even when you have done all you can to redress your failure and transform your life, there will be some who will never trust you and never give you a second chance. And depending on who those people are, it may really hurt. What you must do is focus on those who choose to forgive, to extend their trust to you once again, and to those who are willing to give you another chance.

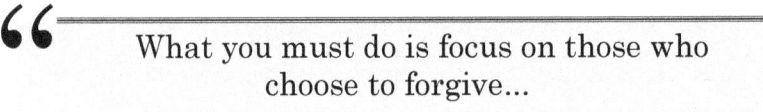

> What you must do is focus on those who choose to forgive...

Honor them in your thoughts, words, and deeds, infusing absolute honesty and integrity into your relationships with these people.

The process of rebuilding your credibility will eventually be fulfilled. It will not happen overnight, and even though it may take some time, you will ultimately attain your goal. **Do not focus on how long the process is taking**. Rather focus on what you are doing today! Consciously choose to do your best and be your best throughout every waking moment.

Remember to keep your heart open to God's direction in your life, even when His instruction seems futile. A story I once heard puts this into perspective. A man received direction from God while in prayer. He was told to go up to this mountain where he would find a large bolder hanging on a ledge. God told him to use his strength to push against this boulder. So the young man journeyed up to the mountain and began to push the boulder. All day long, he pushed with all his might but nothing happened. He went home and the following morning while in prayer, God told him to go back to the ledge on the mountain and to push against the boulder again. Convinced that today would be his day, the young man went up feeling a strong determination to push that boulder over the edge.

He spent all day pushing against the boulder, using all his strength and might, and yet by the end of the day the boulder had not budged. This went on, and as the weeks turned into months, he kept returning to the ledge to push against the boulder. Every day, the young man remained faithful and did what he was told, but still, the boulder never budged a centimeter. Finally, at the end of one day, after using all his strength with no result, he fell on his knees and prayed to God. He told the Lord how faithful he had been these many months, and yet he was simply unable to push this boulder off the ledge. After a moment of deep silence, the young man heard the Lord's reply: "I never asked you to push the boulder off the ledge. I simply asked you to push the boulder." The young man could sense a smile coming forth from God as he sat in a state of confusion. God explained to him that as a result of faithfully obeying what he had been directed to do, he had strengthened his arms and his legs to an extreme seldom experienced by any man, and now he was prepared for the task that God had ordained for Him. **Man's unfaltering obedience to God will always attain the divine objective, however hidden it might seem at the time.**

So remember to keep it simple – just do what God is telling you to do. Don't go running after people in an attempt to gain their favor and have them like you again. Don't assume you have a better way or know a shortcut to rebuilding your credibility. Leave it in God's hands. Be obedient to His Word and His direction. Make good use of the advice given to you in this book. You will wake up one morning, look in the mirror and see reflected in the glass the character of an individual who has been strengthened through an experience. You will smile at the reflection of your refined character and the genuine credibility that exudes from your very pores. You will no longer see the shattered life that was foretold among the broken shards of your failure.

## Your Thoughts...

112  Broken

# Chapter Ten
## Picking Up the Pieces[160]

*"Behold, as the clay is in the potter's hand,
so are ye in mine hand,..."*
— **Jeremiah 18:6**

When I speak of a broken life, I am referring to the consequences of sin. Sin is a form of failure that has eternal ramifications if it is not addressed according to Scripture. While struggling to pick up the pieces of your life, it is important to understand that only the skilled hands of our Lord and Savior can properly deal with many of the issues you will face. Having personally submitted to this process, I find myself completely awed by God's authenticity. God and the Words He has given us for guidance never cease to amaze me! It does not matter what you are going through or what you may have been through, His holy Word always presents us with revelation, wisdom and direction.

As previously mentioned, moving forward to a place of restoration is a process that has no timeline, nor time limit. Before we pick up the pieces, let's take a moment to really understand what the concept of a broken life entails. Webster's Dictionary defines broken as, "separated into parts or pieces by violence; disconnected; fractured; cracked, made infirm or weak, crushed and ruined."[161] The Apple Dictionary[162] defines "broken" as an adjective, with sense 1 referring to the following meanings:

1 having been fractured or damaged and no longer in one piece or in working order: a broken arm.
- rejected, defeated, or despairing : he went to his grave a broken man | a broken heart.
- sick or weakened : broken health.
- (of a relationship) ended, typically by betrayal or faithlessness : a broken marriage.
- disrupted or divided : broken families.
- (of an agreement or promise) not observed by one of the parties involved.

> This is the battle between what God expects us to do and what we desire to do.

The Apostle Paul spoke about a war that continuously played out in his mind as his spirit fought against his flesh. This is the battle between what God expects us to do and what we desire to do. This conflict is brutal and when we do what is contrary to God's Word, we eventually find ourselves broken into pieces. Just as the Webster's Dictionary defines this process, we are separated into pieces through the violence of failure. Envision your life as a precious vessel that is picked up and thrown against the wall. The end result is a shattered vase strewn across the floor. This image reflects the life of one who has failed God. But when we give our lives to Jesus and follow His commands for salvation, *"we have this treasure in earthen vessels, that the excellency of the power may be of God, and not of us."*[163] This is the hope and promise we should desire to obtain – the Spirit of God within us.

This phase of the process will have you taking a moment to look at the broken pieces of your life and discerning where each piece came from within the structure of your life. You will quickly realize there are pieces that have been shattered into tiny fragments, unusable and impossible to reconnect with other pieces. These represent your character and integrity. The idea of putting these pieces back into their restored place

> 66 "...the idea of restoring your character and integrity on your own is simply impossible."

just using your own abilities will never materialize into reality. Without drawing on the power of God and the guidance given in His Word, the idea of restoring your character and integrity is simply impossible to achieve. Recognizing this important truth is crucial to your ultimate restoration.

Following on from this indispensable step, you may start examining the larger pieces, which can represent close family members or other loved ones. These larger pieces may be reconnected to the other parts of your shattered life, but you may well find scar tissue present along the edges. These raised ridges might be blemished and cracked from the strain of the relationship, yet in most cases these pieces will at least still be there. Finally, you will find some remaining pieces that are not so easily recognizable... these you have to be very careful with! They will have sharp edges that can easily cut you if you attempt to handle them carelessly. These may represent so-called friends and others who will quickly use your failure to hurt you, either for their own gain or as a means of retribution against you.

Each piece represents something significant, and yet it may not actually be necessary for your life. Some of those pieces that made up who you were and what you did are flaws or blemishes within your nature that have diminished your value. Remember what God said to Jeremiah concerning Israel: *"Behold, as the clay is in the potter's hand, so are ye in mine hand,..."* Using our own wisdom or talent, we can never pick up the pieces of our brokenness to become whole and new again. But, when we allow ourselves to be the clay that is shaped into a vessel by our Potter, Jesus Christ, we are given the opportunity to be recreated into a superior vessel. **This promise from God requires a simple prerequisite from you: placing your faith in Jesus Christ.** In addition to your faith in Christ, you also need to cultivate an understanding that there is an enemy of your soul who does not want you to use the measure of faith that God has given to you:

*"The thief cometh not, but for to steal, and to kill, and to destroy: I am come that they might have life, and that they might have it more abundantly." –* John 10:10 (KJV)

Within the Book of Jeremiah you will find nuggets of Scriptural gold to increase the faith already residing within you. Jeremiah is called by God to visit the local Potter's house. Jeremiah obediently goes and watches while the Potter works with his clay. As the Potter shaped his clay into a vessel, we are told that it was "marred"[164] in his hands, and yet he did not discard his work. The potter could easily have thrown this disfigured vessel into his pile of previously flawed works. Instead, he worked on that messed up clay until he was able to create another vessel that was no longer marred, and with which he was pleased.

**As you turn your life, your failure, and your broken pieces over**

> This process will not only restore you, it will make you whole again.

**to the Master Potter, He will remove the marred areas of your life and turn you into something better.** This process will not only restore you, it will make you whole again. Remember that you cannot do this by yourself – only Jesus can take your imperfections and turn them into a superior vessel that can contain His Holy Spirit. As you trust in Him, God will do this for you.

When the vessel representing your life was thrown violently against the wall, you momentarily stopped in shock, thinking that all your dreams had been shattered. All your hopes and carefully constructed aspirations were irreparably shattered. In that moment, you may have surmised there was no hope of your life ever being put back together again. Perhaps you considered that life was no longer worth living;

> " ...the divine Potter clearly states that even though you may be marred, He is not finished..

that you were not worth the air you breathed; and that your future had just ended. And yet, the divine Potter clearly states that even though you may be marred, He is not finished with you yet. Through your patient obedience to Him, God begins to pick up all your broken pieces, reshaping you, and remolding you with His hands of mercy and grace. He will no doubt put some pressure on certain parts of your life during this process, and it will be painful for a while as the flesh succumbs to the will of the spirit.

As these pieces are being picked up, you may wonder from time to time if this hardship is necessary. You may wonder if you really do have to go through the difficult process of being remodeled, and why it has to take so long. You might even consider the process of remolding to be more painful than the original break. I remember asking God, "Why does this hurt more now, than my original failure?" And once again, He whispered into my life that this pressing and shaping was necessary, and that I was to trust Him through every difficult season and situation in life. Eventually I realized that as long as He carries me in His hands, I have nothing to worry about. **In other words, you need to hang in there and let God do what He needs to do to turn you into the vessel He created you to be.**

Your faith is critical to the process, and so are your actions. God told Jeremiah that as soon as His people, the Israelites, repented, He would remove the judgment being carried out against them for their sins. They had to do their part in order for God to do His. They needed to believe again in the God of Abraham and stop serving other idols. They needed to grasp once again the truth shouted out by Isaiah for all the ages to know: *"Hear O Israel: the LORD our God is one LORD:..."*[165]

Doing your part can be understood through yet another Scriptural illustration. In the Book of Nehemiah, we find a man of God who hears about the condition of his city, Jerusalem, which is in ruins. The walls are broken into pieces and the gates have been consumed with fire. He stood before the king, who noticed that Nehemiah was not himself, and that he seemed very sad.

Nehemiah asked the king if he could be released from service to rebuild the walls and gates of his beloved city. The king granted him permission to go. What Nehemiah did when he arrived, was to investigate the damage for himself. Scripture presents us with a detailed picture of his investigation:

*"And I went out by night by the gate of the valley, even before the dragon well, and to the dung port, and viewed the walls of Jerusalem, which were broken down, and the gates thereof were consumed with fire."* – Nehemiah 2:13 (KJV) (Emphasis added)

In the previous verse, we are informed that Nehemiah did not tell anyone what God had placed in his heart to accomplish concerning the rebuilding of the walled city. I personally believe Nehemiah did not want to be discouraged, nor did he want to be told it would be impossible to do what he planned on doing. The city walls were in ruin... how can one rebuild a crumbled ruin?

> ...do not allow seemingly impossible circumstances to limit you faith in God!

This is where you need to be very careful – do not allow seemingly impossible circumstances to limit your faith in God! In Paul's letter to the Corinthians, he reminds them that as Christians, *"we walk by faith,*

## Chapter Ten: Picking Up The Pieces

*not by sight."*[166] God has placed this book in your hands to guide you into doing your part so that He can rebuild your life from the inside out. There will be those who will tell you that it can never be done, and others who tell you that it will never be the same. This is why I mentioned earlier that you must have faith. You need to seek God first, and pray earnestly in your desire to pick up the pieces of your brokenness.

Nehemiah experienced similar negative confessions from those around him that I have described. Sanballat, Tobiah and Geshem heard what Nehemiah was planning to do, and they laughed at him and mocked him mercilessly.[167] However, their words did not stop him. He took the responsibility of seeing that the walls were rebuilt, especially because many others were depending upon this for their own safety. Nehemiah deeply respected the God he served. He was also profoundly aware of the figure he represented as God's servant on the earth. Being in alignment with the will of God, Nehemiah set his own will to the task of rebuilding the walls and gates of his city, refusing to accept its state of brokenness and disrepair.

These are some of the tools you will need to pick up the pieces of your own life:

- Acknowledge the fact that your are in pieces as a result of your failure.
- Surrender every aspect of your life to God.
- Exercise your God-given faith and apply it to your desire for restoration.
- Let God lead, direct, and work in you, as well as through you.

> This is your responsibility in picking up the pieces - the process starts within you.

This is your responsibility in picking up the pieces – the process starts within you. Whether or not others encourage you through this process, you can be sure they are counting on you to rebuild your life. Especially those close to you. Your brokenness makes them vulnerable and weak. These people may include your children, spouse, siblings or dear friends. Whoever they are, you need to do this for them as well as for yourself. And remember, you are a child of God. **You are a vessel that He has made and is shaping into a temple that His spirit can reside within.** It is therefore up to you to go out and do what is necessary to see that every piece of your life is picked up and placed before God, so He can perform His miraculous intervention on the Potter's wheel.

## Your Thoughts...

## Broken

# Chapter Eleven
## Focus on Your Everyday Successes[168]

*"Brethren, I count not myself to have apprehended: but this one thing I do, forgetting those things which are behind, and reaching forth unto those things which are before,..."*
– **Philippians 3:13**

Your continued progress of moving from that place of failure and defeat to a position of full restoration will depend upon how you choose to focus your time and energy. The worst thing you can do at this point is to worry about past failures.

> **"** The worst thing you can do at this point is to worry about past failures.

It will only compound into yet more failures in the future. This is why the Apostle Paul wrote that we must forget *"those things which are behind."* This was his secret to success and it can be ours as well. Picking up the pieces means to focus on the good parts of your life, the things that are salvageable and productive for your future. You must leave the mistakes and failures behind and focus on how you can do better at this very moment, and moving forward.

Consider this for a moment. The Bible has taught us that if we concentrate on our present problems and spend our time wallowing in the failures of the past, this exercise becomes self-destructive to our being. The victory that Jesus Christ gained in overcoming sin would never have happened if He had focused on the struggle involved, and the possibility of failure. The greatest victory ever achieved was the result of Jesus focusing on the future and what would be achieved through His earthly ministry. In his humanity, Jesus understood the emotions that can

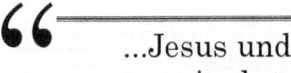
> ...Jesus understood the emotions that can cripple one with fear and doubt.

cripple one with fear and doubt. He also understood the psychological aspects related to human emotions that can produce serious bouts of depression. Yet, Jesus saw the greater purpose that He came to earth for and did not allow anything or anyone to sway Him from his purpose.

You have been created for such a time as this. You have been introduced to some of the key writers and individuals of the Holy Bible who sinned and failed God, yet were able to move past their failures and become pivotal to the work of the Kingdom. Regardless of what has transpired in your life and what you have done, you are not wiped out, washed up, doomed, or forever finished. **You have had a setback concerning where God wants you to be.** You have allowed your own humanity to supersede God's will for your life, but it's still not too late to walk in the Father's will. You are standing up now, and being called to leave those failures behind. You are being called to reach *"forth unto those things which are before."* You may be thinking at this moment, "easier said than done" and you are right, especially if you are looking to the end result, rather than where you stand right now. The place you currently occupy, when compared to the place of restoration you desire to inhabit, may seem to be a very long way off and unachievable, but let me remind you that, *"...greater is he that is in you, than he that is in the world."*[169] The spirit of God will guide you moment-by-moment and day-by-day to that place of restoration. He will lead and direct you as you place your trust in Him. It is like running a marathon where God is your coach.

When an individual who has never run a race before plans to run a twenty-six-mile marathon, he does not proceed without any preparation or guidance. In fact, when this individual begins their journey, they may be lucky – the first time out – to make it around the block once! There is a plan that is put into place by the coach to aid in accomplishing the goal set by the runner. The plan always requires the runner to focus on today and what can be realistically achieved. For example, the runner may begin by just completing a brisk walk on that first day, which may only be one mile in distance. Yet, every day the focus is on that day only. At the end of each day one will either celebrate what they accomplished or look at why they did not meet their daily goal, and adjust their training regimen accordingly. Each day is focused on pushing a little further ahead. Eventually, having trained with commitment, discipline, and perseverance, the runner will stand at the starting line of their twenty-six-mile marathon to run their race.

Restoration will not happen overnight, but like a marathon, it will be accomplished over time if you too remain diligent in your efforts, stay the course, and build on what you have accomplished each day. I will admit that from the outset, the journey can oftentimes seem lonely and the finish line too far away. I personally know there is no way I could have made it to where I am today if my focus had been on the final results. I had to take it one day at a time, and there were times where I found myself only able to focus on just one moment at a time.

My personal desire was to be restored in both a public and private manner. Publicly, I hoped to once again serve in leadership through ministry. Privately, I wanted to rebuild my life upon the Godly principles of character and integrity. This meant I would no longer accept working in the 'gray' areas of life. It meant that my words and deeds would

> ...my words and deeds would magnify God, rather than bringing shame to Him...

magnify God, rather than bringing shame to Him, to my family and my friends. Starting out, I thought I would succeed in running a twenty-six-mile marathon before I would ever see myself restored to such a place, living my life in the manner I now live.

I began by breaking down the things I could accomplish one day at a time – doable action steps. I began with prayer each day, and would then move on to reading my Bible. In my actions, I would hold to that time-tested acronym, WWJD: What Would Jesus Do? I would ask myself that question each time something came up, and then respond accordingly. At the end of the day, I would thank God for every success and repent

> " ...I would thank God for every success and repent for any area where I came up short.

for any area where I came up short. I also made myself accountable to my wife and close ministerial elders. I remained honest to them and accepted and submitted to their authority, because I knew they had my best interest at heart. Each day built upon the day before and as the days turned into weeks, my life was strengthened through the Spirit of God, as I praised Him for every success and thanked Him for every second chance.

Focusing on the everyday successes can be broken down into the three foundational areas I identified as necessary for a marathon runner: commitment, discipline, and perseverance. As you begin to create a mental picture of that place of restoration for your life, you will want to utilize these three tools if you truly desire to achieve success one day at a time.

One very important factor that must be addressed from the outset is to sharpen your daily focus on those things within the scope of your own control. **It is pointless to focus on the aspects of life that are outside the sphere of your control – what others are saying or doing has no bearing on the success of your restoration.** Your commitment, discipline, and perseverance will be doomed before you can even start if you choose to focus on the opinions of other people concerning your progress. Just as no other person can train for the marathon runner, so can no other person fulfill your own obligation to this journey. As you begin to build on all three of these areas each day, I know from personal experience and from God's promises that you will be ensured daily successes, which will cumulatively lead you to that place of restoration God has for you.

## COMMITMENT

Without your heart, mind, and soul focused on where you want to be, you will never achieve your desired goal. You must be committed

> You must be committed to today in bringing about the changes necessary to your own...

to today in bringing about the changes necessary to your own personal growth in character and integrity . This can only be accomplished as you look to God as the Author and Finisher of your faith. Beginning with today, you should focus on committing this day to God. He desires that we commit ourselves totally to him, holding nothing back. This means that it is not our will, but His will that must be established instead of our agendas, hopes, plans, achicvements, desires, thoughts, and habits. In other words, everything must be turned over to him for this day and every day going forward.

You can do this by first acknowledging that you have been created and that He is your Creator. Everything in the universe is His and without Him you can do nothing of value. Then acknowledge that all that you have already belongs to God. My day starts by giving God thanks for the day, and giving thanks for who He is and all He is doing in and through me. I then present myself totally to Christ and ask Him to do His work in me. As I move through the details of my day, I seek ways to give God praise for what I have and what He is doing in my life and the lives of others. It is as simple as thanking Him for my breakfast, and giving God

> It is as simple as thanking Him for my breakfast...

praise in the knowledge that all I have is because of Him. The Book of Proverbs even states, "*In all thy ways acknowledge Him,...*"[170] The term, "ways" refers to a journey, a path, and a way of life.

Therefore, in your daily journey, make sure that your path is guided by Christ and every aspect of your life reflects the goodness of God.

Begin your day committed to making it your best! This happens naturally when you start the day with prayer. This will help you to focus your mind as you consider what you wish to accomplish during each day. **Remain committed, no matter what distractions you may encounter, and never give up!** You may forget a day or mess up in some other way, but remain committed to the process. When an athlete falls, he may roll once or twice, but he or she immediately jumps up again if not injured. An athlete will run whether the sun is scorching his face or the heavens open up and pour out buckets of rain. The weather has no effect on such an athlete, and neither does he allow his feelings to prevent him from training – he's committed.

**DISCIPLINE**

> Discipline is what we need most, but what we want the least.

Discipline is what we need most, but what we want the least. If we are honest with ourselves, knowing what to do is not usually the problem...

it is having the discipline to do what is right with which we often struggle. Whether you are trying to prevent yourself from succumbing to fleshly desires that lead to moral impurity, or if you are prioritizing the important things in life over those that are urgent – discipline is a key character necessary to producing the fruit of the spirit. It doesn't matter what you are dealing with on a daily basis, discipline is crucial to your eventual success. We all look in the mirror and think we could be doing more, doing better, but find ourselves lacking. It's because one of the hardest things to do in life is to change. We are creatures of habit! We find change very strenuous. **Cultivating change in our daily lives is one of the most overwhelming and difficult tasks that any of us face.**

In my own testimony, I shared my character flaws that were developed when I was young. Flaws that were engrained in me over the years. It is really difficult for us humans to suddenly change habits that have been a part of our nature for long periods of time. I learned through my own failure that I had to begin by saying 'no' to my own desires – the flesh is very strong-willed and it takes rugged self-denial to overcome the flesh. Discipline is critical to your success. In changing my life habits, I had to learn how to order my life in a certain way, which helped me to override the undisciplined nature that was so much a part of my being. When training for a marathon, an athlete must train his body to operate at optimum for the race he or she plans to run. Similarly, you must learn to train your spirit through the power of the Holy Spirit so you can pursue what is good and righteous through Christ.

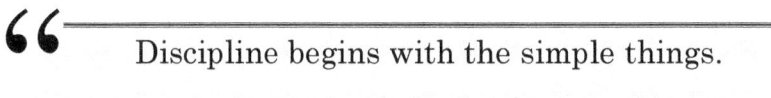
> Discipline begins with the simple things.

Discipline begins with the simple things. Begin your day in prayer and reading the Word of God. It is not about how long you spend praying or how much Bible text you read at this stage. It's about setting the time aside to do this, and to do it faithfully every day. As you commit and discipline yourself to rigorously take these two action steps on a daily basis, you will find that your relationship with God will improve. In time, the depth and breadth of your prayer life and reading will increase naturally. Once you are in the habit of spending quality time with God,

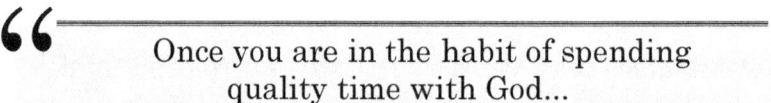
> Once you are in the habit of spending quality time with God...

you can begin to address any bad habits you may have acquired, as well as those aspects of your life that brought you to a state of brokenness. Challenge yourself at the start of each new day to become more Christ-like, rebuking the bad habits and destructive actions that initiated your failure.

Focus on acquiring Biblically sound habits which in turn produce positive actions. Remember that the habits acquired over a long period of time have become a part of your nature, so changing these habits may take some time. Take small steps. Each time you successfully overcome self-destructive behavior, or you manage to reinforce positive patterns of behavior, you should give God praise and celebrate that success. You have not arrived, but you've taken a step in the right direction. Over time, you will find yourself moving in this new direction, the Bible-based direction that leads to restoration. Just as the athlete training for a marathon accomplishes his desired goal by adding miles to his training regimen, so must you continue to add positive habits and actions to your own regimen for success.

### PERSEVERANCE

When we consider the men and women of the Bible, we see that some of the greatest successes in their lives were achieved in spite of seemingly insurmountable odds. For these men and women, it was

> ...Noah, who persevered for more than one hundred and twenty years building an ark...

perseverance that produced success in their lives. Let me remind you of Noah, who persevered for more than one hundred and twenty years in building an ark, while surrounded by corrupt and contemptuous unbelievers. In a similar vein, Moses showed great perseverance while leading the Israelites through the wilderness. He persevered for forty years due to their unbelief.

**You have begun a journey that you cannot quit. You cannot quit on yourself!** There are people that you do not know, and most likely will never know, who are praying for you. Praying for your success; your restoration; your life; and your soul. As I write these words, I am praying for you. I do not know your name or your story, but I am praying for you, and I am committed to praying every day for you. For God knows you and what you need, and He places your burdens into the hearts of His prayer warriors all around the world. You are running your own race, but you are not alone. **God will have people stationed along your path to cheer you on.** A phone call, text, or letter from an old friend or family member will reach you just when you need it most.

Words of encouragement, a peaceful place in which to rest, and even a laugh or two, will give you the strength and joy to continue along your new chosen path. These moments of respite from the struggle of daily life will become your rest stops.

Thomas Edison said, "Many of life's failures are people who did not realize how close they were to success when they gave up."[171] Perseverance is a steady persistence in moving forward, regardless of the difficulties or discouragements that one may face. Keep your eye on the prize and know that if others can make it to that place of restoration, so can you.

Focus on your everyday successes – you have successfully completed this chapter and you can celebrate this accomplishment by thanking God for the knowledge and guidance you gleaned from these pages. As you begin to put these points into practice, you will find you are closer today to that victory than you were yesterday!

## Your Thoughts...

# Chapter Twelve
## The Restoration of A Failure – A Biblical Perspective[172]

*"The steps of a good man are ordered by the Lord: and he delighteth in his way. 24 Though he fall, he shall not be utterly cast down: for the Lord upholdeth him with his hand."*
– **Psalm 37:23-24 (KJV)**

Understanding failure from a Biblical perspective is very important to our growth in Christ. When speaking of failure, it is necessary to distinguish between the failure to be chosen for a football team, and a moral failure, which results from sin. Both types of failure will produce the potential for growth. The person who experiences the disappointment of not being chosen to represent their local football team may feel shame, bitterness, or anger, but no spiritual repercussions will necessarily result from this failure. This individual will soon realize that railing against the coach's decision not to include them in the team is totally futile. Once they have calmed down, they will recognize the need to improve their skills on the football field, or to increase their level of fitness. This recognition will allow them the opportunity for growth – either by improving their skill, or increasing their level of fitness. Or both! Failure resulting from sin offers a similar opportunity for that individual to experience growth ,

> Failure resulting from sin offers a similar opportunity for that individual ...

and yet sin always produces consequences. Even if it serves only to reinforce the pattern of sinfulness in their life.

This may seem insignificant, but just as neural pathways in the human brain are reinforced and strengthened by repetition,[173] so do patterns of sin become more intricately intertwined into our human spirits through repetition.

King David is a perfect example of how a seemingly minor indiscretion was finally fulfilled in the death of his son. For "the wages of sin" – once sinfulness has worked through or completed its cycle – "is death"[174] Allow me to elaborate on this explanation one more time. At "the time when kings go forth to battle," King David "sent Joab, and his servants with him, and all Israel;" but "David tarried still at Jerusalem."[175] By removing himself from the field of battle, David made a decision to renege on his duty as king. In our modern world, we may well consider this a minor indiscretion, but it was this first mistake that allowed David the freedom to indulge in his second mistake. As commander of Israel's army, David was just as strictly bound to the soldiers' code of conduct during a time of war – the usual comforts of life, such as lavish meals and sexual relations, were withheld from men at war. They renounced these by choice, saving their strength and keeping their focus for battle. David was aware of this, because when he was being chased by King Saul, he took his men to the priest at Nob, hoping for some provisions. The priest, Ahimelech, only had consecrated bread to offer them, but asked first if the young men had "kept themselves at least from women."[176] In those early days, David knew the value of abstinence during war, and by following the protocol of an Israelite soldier, he was granted, along with his men, the sustenance of "hallowed bread."[177]

We know, from the details given in chapter four, that during this time of idleness while his army was at war, King David noticed Bathsheba bathing on a rooftop below him. Instead of turning his gaze, the king settled in to enjoy the show. In that moment, he indulged in the sin of lust, followed quickly by the sin of coveting another man's wife. One seemingly minor indiscretion (tarrying in Jerusalem) soon led to the committing of two sins simultaneously: lust and covetousness. He then extended his thought pattern into a pattern of words, by calling for Bathsheba. Finally, his thoughts, which had turned to words, followed on to the next logical step: he acted upon his thoughts, committing adultery with Bathsheba, the wife of one of his soldiers. Bear with me, for to understand how you can reach a place of restoration, you need to recognize the steps which lead human beings into that depraved state requiring restoration. This will enable you to guard against it in the future. The process of

> The process of restoration includes repentence...

restoration includes repentance, while repentance involves recognizing sin and then developing strategies to turn away from that specific sin whenever you are confronted by it.

Sin always escalates in scale – it never diminishes of its own accord. Only a conscious decision on the part of a believer will reduce the occurrence of sin. When Bathsheba informed the king of her pregnancy, David was caught up in an escalating drama of sin, each deed compounded by the next. He sent for her husband, Uriah, pretending he wanted to be updated on the war being waged by his army, when his actual intention was to entice Uriah to sleep with his wife. This would squash any questions about her pregnancy. Unable to reduce Uriah to his own depraved state (Uriah refused to lay with his wife), David plots the death of this loyal soldier. Uriah was killed, according to plan, and David thought he was off the hook. Instead, the son born to him by Bathsheba, who was born as a result of the king's sin, died because of his father's compounded sins.

Do you see the pattern? A minor indiscretion leads to lust and covetousness. These lead to adultery, which finally leads to murder, followed by the death of David's newborn son. The wages of sin... Seldom do we fail in one spectacular, stupid step. We lead ourselves to death one sin at a time. Perhaps the most interesting part of this story is David's

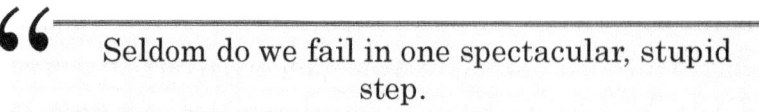
> Seldom do we fail in one spectacular, stupid step.

knowledge of God's mercy. He fasts and prays for seven days in the hope of God's anger at his sin being turned away.[178] Yet God's master plan for the future of humanity did not include a child born from the depraved rationale experienced by David during this time of weakness. The lineage of the Messiah was at stake! Only after the child died did this final step of David's failure become clear to all of Israel. Only then is the king able to initiate his path to restoration. God's forgiveness is granted, but the consequences of David's actions change his life forever. His kingdom was rife with violence thereafter, and he later experienced unutterable anguish in a time that was meant to be the golden years of his life.

What can we draw from David's experience? Well, considering that he was a man after God's own heart,[179] it becomes evident that sin is virtually inevitable[180] through the course of human life. We are predisposed[181] to a sinful life . It can be avoided, but this entails some

> We are predisposed to a sinful life.

basic knowledge of how to recognize the steps leading to sin, and how to nip it in the bud of its germination. The reason I have taken time to point this out is to emphasize the importance of this knowledge while undergoing the process of restoration. Forewarned is forearmed, as the saying goes. Chapter four pointed to the beginning of King David's restoration, which started with David worshipping the Lord.[182] David had the wisdom to understand that no matter how far he had fallen, God would allow him to follow a path to restoration.

The problem with sin is that ordinary mortals are not always as forgiving as God. David never did command the same respect he had worked so hard to earn. Imagine how Joab felt, the commander of

 *The problem with sin is that ordinary mortals are not always as forgiving as God.*

David's army, who David had involved in the murder of Uriah. How could he possibly respect his king after being used like a pawn to achieve David's satisfaction. Joab later killed Absalom, David's son, against King David's clearly expressed wish.[183] Even though the king repented, and turned away from the wickedness which bred a slew of sins during his time of idleness, he continued to reap the wages of his sin. I am being blunt because I want you to understand that even though God willingly restores those who seek restoration from Him, there are spiritual laws attached to sin that God Himself cannot – or at least, chooses not – to circumvent. **Blood must be shed to pay the price of sin, and this is why Jesus was given to die on the cross in the place of sinful human beings.**

So what does the Bible say about the restoration of those who have failed? What I can tell you is that in all things God works for the good of those who love Him.[184] God's grace is constantly at work in our lives. The Apostle Peter is an excellent example of this principle. Jesus knew in advance that Peter would deny Him three times on the night of His illegal trial. Does this mean that Peter was destined by God to fall pray to this specific sin? No! But God operates outside of our human construction of linear time. God knew without any doubt that Peter would succumb to this particular sin. Of all the possible outcomes that Peter was presented with in that moment, God knew he would choose to deny his association with Jesus three times. **The Creator of the universe is not bound by time.** C.S. Lewis sums up this concept brilliantly in his book, Mere Christianity. The chapter is called, TIME AND BEYOND TIME:

*Almost certainly God is not in Time. His life does not consist of moments following one another. If a million people are praying to Him at ten-thirty tonight, He need not listen to them all in that one little snippet which we call ten-thirty. Ten-thirty – and every other moment from the beginning of the world – is always the Present for Him. If you like to put it that way, He has all eternity in which to listen to the split second of prayer put up by a pilot as his plane crashes in flames... God is not hurried along in the Time-stream of this universe any more than an author is hurried along in the imaginary time of his own novel. He has infinite attention to spare for each one of us... But God, I believe, does not live in a Time-series at all. His life is not dribbled out moment by moment like ours: with Him it is, so to speak, still 1920 and already 1960. For His life is Himself.*[185]

God in His sovereignty knows in advance the choices we will make, and this is how Jesus knew Peter would succumb to the pressure of denying Him. What Peter learned from this experience, however, is surely an important part of his future leadership among the disciples. To fully understand human failure we must consider three things: divine sovereignty, satanic activity, and human responsibility.[186] Understanding

> Understanding divine sovereignty is recognizing that God controls...

divine sovereignty is recognizing that God controls human governments to achieve His will. [187] Knowing that God is operating on such a grand scale, we begin to grasp that the governing of our lives is a simple task for Him in comparison. Remember that God is beyond time, thereby fully understanding what is best for us, especially those who love and serve Him. Knowing in advance what sins we will commit, God takes into account the measures available to Him to teach us important life lessons.

Through those failures in our lives which result from sin, God is able to reprove and instruct us accordingly, shaping us into vessels that can be used in His service.

Satanic activity is another aspect involved in human sin and failure. Scripture informs us that our *"adversary the devil,"* walks about *"as a roaring lion,... seeking whom he may devour."*[188] Those who love and serve God need not be overly concerned by this, as the devil needs God's permission to attack His children. Jesus made this quite clear, adding that He is interceding on our behalf:

*"And the Lord said, Simon, Simon, behold, Satan hath desired to have you, that he may sift you as wheat: 32 But I have prayed for thee, that thy faith fail not: and when thou art converted, strengthen thy brethren."* – Luke 22:31-32 (KJV)

Jesus knew of Satan's request to "sift" the disciples as wheat. He also knew that because of this satanic pressure, Peter would experience fear, and would suffer a lapse of integrity in denying his association with Christ. In short, Jesus knew Peter would fail... but, He also knew that Peter's ultimate faith in Christ would not fail, and that this experience would serve to strengthen Peter's faith, and in turn would serve to strengthen his fellow disciples. The following paragraph aptly sums up the fact that Peter's sin of denial was incorporated into God's plan and purpose for his life:

Theologians would say that Peter's denial was included in the eternal decree of God, purposed before the beginning of time. When Peter failed, he did not thrust himself outside of the purpose (or decree) of God, but continued within it. God's program for man's redemption, His purposes for the church, for the Apostles, and especially for Peter were not suddenly set aside by Peter's sin. God's plans for Peter were realized both in spite of and because of Peter's sin.[189]

This concept is well grounded in Scripture. Remember how Joseph's brothers feared his reaction to their father Jacob's death? They were afraid that the wrong they had done to Joseph by selling him into slavery would be avenged now that their father was dead. But Joseph had acquired great wisdom through the trials he had suffered. He had learned that God uses the sins of human beings to create the potential for blessings:

> ...Joseph had acquired great wisdom through the trials he had suffered.

*"But as for you, ye thought evil against me; but God meant it unto good, to bring to pass, as it is this day, to save much people alive."* – Genesis 50:20 (KJV)

Joseph recognized that God had turned the sin of his brothers into a means of saving Israel (and Egypt) from death by famine. He recognized that not only does God permit sin, but He purposes to include it in His eternal plan.[190] **God uses our failures and our sins to shape us into vessels useful to His purposes.** While Satan has the capacity to tempt us into sin, it is how we respond to temptation that either strengthens our faith or causes us to fail. But even in failure God is able to restore us to righteousness – yet this does not rid us of the fact that our lives will probably still reflect the consequences of our sin.

Even though Satan seeks to destroy us, God allows him to oppose us for our strengthening and advancement in the faith.[191] This concept is clearly outlined by the Apostle Paul's *"thorn in the flesh."*[192] The strength of Christ *"is made perfect"* in human weakness.[193] Sin is permitted so we can experience failure. Human failure is experienced so we can develop our faith and trust in God. Failure is neither accidental nor incidental to Christian growth; it is essential.[194]

Having considered how divine sovereignty and satanic activity play different roles in our understanding of human failure, we now turn to the role played by human responsibility. Human beings need to accept the fact that we are prone to making both good and bad choices, which produce either good or bad consequences. Even though Peter

> ...need to accept the fact that we are prone to making both good and bad choices...

was warned to guard against the temptation of denying Christ, he was paralyzed by fear in the moment of his temptation, and consequently made fear-based choices rather than choices based on the truth of his integrity.

Thankfully God knows in advance the choices we will make, and is therefore able to plan our restoration to follow our failure. During His final meal with His disciples, Jesus told Peter he would deny knowing Him three times before the sun rose.[195] The interesting thing about this statement is that it is made in answer to Peter's bold proclamation that he was "*ready to go with*" Jesus, "*both into prison, and to death.*"[196] In spite of Peter's resolve to follow his Lord into prison and to death, he later realized that he needed a power greater than his own human effort to excel in his role of discipleship. He had learned the lesson that he could not trust his own will, but had to rely completely on God if he was to accomplish God's will.

What is the main difference between one who has failed dismally and suffered personal disgrace, and one who has never experienced the ignominy of public failure? Humility! That is the major difference in nine cases out of ten. **The humiliation of failure is a very effective cure for pride, and there is no quality more necessary for leadership than that of humility.** [197] God takes the predominant (and often recurring) failures of our lives and He shapes them into useful tools with which we can serve Him in the advancement of His kingdom.

When I consider my own failure, I realize it was humility that brought me to this place, where I am able to take the time to share my restoration process with others. It would be much easier and more comforting for me to keep my past failure hidden, never to be discussed. However, when I speak at a conference, minister in a church or even when speaking to individuals, I will at times use the opportunity to share my testimony. As I dredge up all the old pain, and the awful consequence of my failure, I am struck again by the reality that only God's grace has enabled me to share my experiential knowledge. His grace gave me the hope to become a remolded vessel, useful to the advancement of His kingdom. What was meant to destroy me, God used as an opportunity. He allowed me, in my newfound humility, to start seeking Him in earnest. And when a person

> " *What was meant to destroy me, God used as an opportunity.*

starts to earnestly seek God, they soon begin to grow in Him. God used my failure to mold me into an instrument from which others may draw strength and hope in dealing with their own failure.

Let us once again consider the Apostle Peter. Peter's smug, self-confident arrogance was eventually shaped by God into bold humility. Consider Peter's gentle words of counsel to his fellow-elders in the opening verses of his first epistle.[198] Peter had learned through the fiery trials of his failure that it is wisest to: "*Humble yourselves therefore under the mighty hand of God, that he may exalt you in due time.*"[199] Over time, Peter learned to trust God, not because he figured out a way to avoid sin, but because he took advantage of the lessons presented to him through the process of his restoration. **Peter's sin did not impair his ministry; it prepared him for ministry, by teaching him not to trust in self, but in God.** [200]

We do know that Peter went through a process of restoration. After denying Jesus for the third time, Peter heard the cock crow, and as if on cue, we are told that "*the Lord turned, and looked upon Peter.*"[201] Following on from Peter's recognition of his failure after the eye contact he experienced with Jesus, Scripture informs us that, *"Peter went out, and wept bitterly."*[202] Peter's remorse evidently led to his repentance, which in turn led to his restoration. During the third appearance of Jesus to his disciples after His resurrection, Jesus goes through the process of reinstating Peter to the position of leadership with which he was entrusted. Jesus counters Peter's three denials by encouraging him to negate these denials with three affirmations of his love for Jesus.[203] In reaffirming his love for Jesus, Peter accepted his role as the one who would lead the way in feeding the lambs and the sheep of Christ's flock.

Most of the great men and women of God depicted throughout the Bible suffered various forms of failure. The majority of these failures occurred because they relied on their own solutions to the problems confronting them, rather than relying on God. Because God understands that human failure through sin is inevitable, He incorporates our failings into the life lessons He expects us to learn. For our part, perhaps the most important aspect of the restoration process we should understand

> ...understand...each of us are predisposed to certain patterns of sinfulness.

is that each of us are predisposed to certain patterns of sinfulness. It is in overcoming these patterns that we forge the necessary tools with which to accomplish God's will in our lives and in the lives of those to whom we minister. As expressed earlier in this chapter, sin usually follows a specific process: we first think about committing a sin; which is most often followed by an internal dialogue or a verbal discussion justifying the sin in our own minds; after which we act upon the sinful thought. Thoughts turn to words, which turn to deeds. The simplest method of breaking this pattern is to arrest every negative or sinful thought the moment it enters your conscious mind. This enables you to nip the problem even before it buds. This concept is Scripturally based, and is perhaps the most effective way of governing your thoughts, words and deeds, because it strikes at the root of the process:

*"Casting down imaginations, and every high thing that exalteth itself against the knowledge of God, and bringing into captivity every thought to the obedience of Christ;..."* – 2 Corinthians 10:5 (KJV) (Emphasis added)

A helpful supplement to this process is to meditate on the Word of God after taking captive any sinful thoughts, which helps to establish positive neural pathways in your brain and Godly patterns of obedience within your spirit. God fully understands our human frailty – He watched His own beloved Son suffer all the temptations to which humanity is exposed. Knowing this, we can be confident that He has built into His master plan for our lives effective methods of rising again after we have fallen. This concept is beautifully illustrated in the Book of Psalms:

***"The Lord upholdeth all that fall, and raiseth up all those that be bowed down."*[204]**

## Your Thoughts...

148 Broken

# Chapter Thirteen
## The Role of Leadership in Restoration [205]

*"Brethren, if a man be overtaken in a fault, ye which are spiritual, restore such an one in the spirit of meekness; considering thyself, lest thou also be tempted."*
– **Galatians 6:1**

This chapter may seem somewhat controversial to some, while others might consider that it does not fit very well with the rest of the information presented. However, I find it to be of critical importance, especially if the broken are to be given any hope of being restored and made whole again. I know from personal experience how difficult it is to walk the path to restoration without the love and guidance of spiritual leadership. This chapter is dedicated to and provided for the leadership within the body of Christ, and to those who aspire to assist the fallen. The information contained within this chapter is to be shared in a manner that will bring *"forth therefore fruits meet for repentance:..."*[206]

>  The process of restoration cannot easily be accomplished by any single individual!

The process of restoration cannot easily be accomplished by any single individual! For this process to be most efficient, the guiding hands of spiritually mature leaders are required. Those leaders must have the desire to be instruments for the fulfillment of Scripture in the lives of people seeking mercy and forgiveness. My desire is to bring attention to the Biblical necessity of restoration and the critical role that leadership must play throughout this process.

In more than twenty years of pastoring, I have counseled and guided many through their own failures. My expertise in helping those who failed did not come from my mentors or leaders – the very people I looked to when I was broken. Rather, my knowledge was acquired from various sources: Scripture; academic studies and training; the counsel of a few wise men of God; how I personally envisioned and hoped my own process of restoration might have taken place; and, in addition to the above sources, how I understood the public view and process of restoration. When it comes to this resurrecting power of restoration, sadly, in many cases, the church has fallen short.

> When it comes to this resurrecting power of restoration…the chuch has fallen short.

The church is too often seen as more critical and less forgiving than organizations not affiliated to a church. **It is the Church (the body of Christ) that should be recognized as the true instrument of God's grace ,** as church members reach out to the broken, offering hope, healing, and restoration. If we take a moment to consider some public figures, such as Michael Vick, Tiger Woods, David Letterman, and Martha Stewart, we recognize that each of them had their own personal failures. Being public figures, their failures were catapulted into the public arena. As a result of their public status, their failures were magnified and scrutinized by the press and general public. Irrespective of what each of these private individuals had done – whether they had broken the law, had an adulteress affair, or messed up in some other way – their public stories became the talk of the evening news, and their lives were reduced to interesting topics of debate on various public talk shows. The nasty details of their private lives were publicized, sensationalized, and in short, their reputations were scandalized. However, based on the steps these individuals took, the public forgave them. Each of them had their own personal, yet public comeback – their restoration. **Yet, how often does one hear of the spirit of forgiveness and the power of restoration demonstrated within the church among church members who have fallen?**

When I was dealing with my own personal failure, I worked under the authority of an organization that served as an umbrella for the administration of ministers. My view of the leadership within this organization was negatively influenced by the lack of spiritual fruit I witnessed firsthand, specifically in the areas of forbearance, kindness, goodness, and faithfulness.[207] I also perceived that the leadership were holding to a double standard in certain practices. Let me qualify this statement by saying that my personal views are based upon my own experiences at the hands of these leaders, my emotional state at the time of my personal failure, and my reflections after the failure, which were further influenced by the many who I counseled in my own ministry. My comments, therefore, are by no means aimed at casting a disparaging net over the many good men and women of God, nor the organizations they represent, but rather to draw attention to the powerful influence leadership has in either demonstrating the power of God's grace, or the negative nature of humanity's fallen state.

In my own personal experience, I heard this strong voice that preached and promoted the drawing of sinners to Christ, the forgiveness of sins, and the power of restoration available to sinners. I also saw these principles applied and demonstrated through the process of reaching out to sinners. The contradiction became apparent when I realized that for those who were already saved, such grace was not extended to those who fell. In my counseling, too often I have listened to the stories of those who were ostracized, shunned, and even cast out of the church because of the sin that was made public in their lives. I could personally identify with their hurt and anger as they saw such hypocrisy in their struggle to turn back to God.

When I went through my own personal failure, I was not given the same mercy I saw extended to the influential or well connected. There was a preferential covering given to the privileged that was truly unbiblical. As a result, seeds of bitterness and anger were produced in the less privileged as each fallen individual experienced this double standard. In my case, when meeting with this group of leaders, they offered no plan to assist me in my own restorative process.

Instead, I experienced a strong hand of judgment that even sought to attack those who walked at my side in the spirit of Barnabas. I was shunned and even to this day, I am still marked as an outcast by some. I am thankful as I reflect upon this that these individuals number in the few and do not represent the larger body of Godly leaders I am blessed to interact with.

As I have already presented through Scripture, Bible history is littered with stories of failure by God's people. Scattered throughout the Old and New Testaments, the failure of individuals who were close to God is overwhelming. To the average observer, these accounts can be frighteningly sobering. Even more astounding, however, is the fact that God truly is in the restoration business, clearly demonstrated by His restorative works described throughout the Bible. Time and time again, the Lord takes that broken vessel and makes it brand new. Let there

> Time and time again, the Lord takes that broken vessel and makes it brand new.

be no doubt, the potential for restoration clearly exists throughout the Bible.

Before we delve into a discussion on the role of leadership within the restoration process, let me expound upon a danger in which the church often places itself – or more specifically, certain leaders within particular congregations. The church has been labeled too often as the hypocrite

> "People who condemn others tend to have short-term memories of their own failures."
> – Rev. Robert Martin[208]

and its ministers identified as modern day Pharisees and Scribes. This happens when specific individuals within the church experience public failure through sin, and their path to restoration is dictated by their status or influence. For example, let's consider that the sins of a certain individual in the church become known, but this knowledge is swept under the rug and the person is quickly absolved of their sin by church leadership. When other church members question why this individual was not held rigorously to the process of restoration, they usually discover that either their wealth or influence have negotiated an easy settlement for them.

Rather than leadership insisting that this individual follow the path of repentance to their ultimate restoration, they are given a free pass due to the recognition that they are generous financial benefactors of the church. Other examples may reveal that the individual has a personal or professional relationship with the Pastor or others in leadership, and this becomes the motivating factor for their rapid restoration. This can clearly be identified as hypocritical to God's law of restoration, particularly when considered in the light of Scripture, which explicitly tells us that "God is no respecter of persons."[209] These double standards should never be acceptable.

Grace should be extended to all in the same measure. How the individual who has sinned responds to that grace in his or her own life is what essentially dictates the gift of restoration. As leaders, we must always forgive the offender as Christ has forgiven us. We do not have the authority to identify one sin as being greater than another. Neither do we have the authority to decide that certain vocations or positions of social status have more value than others. **We are required to put into place a Biblical standard and process for restoration.** A process that is rich in love and bathed in mercy, and which marks the doorway through which every broken individual must pass.

Hope for restoration is demonstrated in the Bible. Not only were individuals restored, but whole nations received this grace. When a nation had sinned and God's judgment was pronounced against it, God's Word reveals His mercy, explaining how He erased His initial judgment when that nation humbled itself and repented.[210] Therefore, whether it is a nation or an individual, we in leadership must show the example of Christ. **We must be the instruments for His universal redemptive work, as it is extended to all who have sinned and come short of the glory of God.** [211]

I would like to remind every single church leader that restoration is not only about bringing closure to a sad period in a person's life.[212] Rather, it is about representing the redemptive work of Christ in the life of the broken so they in turn can be restored to a state where they magnify and replicate the mercy of God through their own constructive service to others.

It must be understood from the outset that restoration does not necessarily mean an individual will be brought back to their original position. Whether that position is vocational, a position of social status, or one of relationship, many factors play a part in the restoration

> ...it is their responsiblility to submit to the Biblical mandates dealing with restoration.

process. For those who have failed, it is their responsibility to submit to the Biblical mandates dealing with restoration. Where possible, it is also their responsibility to submit to the love and guidance of spiritually mature leaders whose primary goal is to restore those among us who have fallen.

For leaders, an important prerequisite for ministering to those who have sinned is that they are spiritually mature and that they observe and understand the ministry of Barnabas. Barnabas had the patience and willingness to work with the broken. The Bible illustrates the struggles that the Apostle Paul had with John Mark. He was considered unfaithful and Scripture speaks of how John Mark had previously deserted his fellow brethren in ministry.[213] It was Barnabas who was willing to extend God's mercy by choosing to work with Mark, taking him to Cyprus.[214] We aren't given that much detail of how Barnabas sought to restore Mark's integrity. Yet over time, as a result of this redemptive work, the value of Mark's former ministry was regained, and his capacity as a valuable member of Christ's body was restored to him. Even Paul recognized the new qualities displayed in Mark's behavior by categorically stating his spiritual value: *"Take Mark, and bring him with thee: for he is profitable to me for the ministry."*[215]

The process for restoration begins with five foundational steps.[216] Each step in and of itself does not provide restoration, nor is the leader limited to these only. Based on the specifics of the issue and its surrounding circumstances, additional steps may be required. These additional steps are to be merged into the primary steps. This will ensure that all the issues which have had an impact on the broken, as well as those affected by their failure, are properly and Biblically addressed.

Whether it requires five steps or twenty steps, when this restorative process is melded together in the spirit of love, every piece connected to the other has the power to produce the glorious manifestation of God's work within the life of the individual who has failed. Restoration is literally the fruit of God's grace.

## STEP ONE – HONESTY

This is the first foundational step and must be adhered to by the one who has failed. It must also be encouraged by the leader in a sincere manner that brings hope to the individual. **Restoration hinges on the honesty and transparency of the person who has failed.**

> " Restoration is literally the fruit of God's grace.

They must acknowledge their failure with truth and openness. The sin in one's life can never be addressed if it is not identified as such. This step is similar to that first step taken by an alcoholic who seeks recovery. The very first step is acknowledging their addiction.[217] So must the broken be honest, transparent, and straightforward in speaking about their failure.

Crucial to this first step is the environment in which confession is presented. Firstly, the process must be administered by a leader who is sensitive to the fallen nature of the individual, regardless of the nature of their sin. The leader cannot stand as a judge or jury, nor should they harbor a spirit of condemnation. The environment must be seen as a neutral place where the confessor can experience the cathartic nature of this process. They must feel safe, as this will enable them to experience the heaviness of their past actions being lifted from their spirit as each action or sin is given its rightful name. In other words, this place of confession must offer the sterile safety of a spiritual operating room. The prevailing attitude of the ministering leader must contain absolutely no judgment , as this can easily infect the person seeking restoration, perhaps even causing greater harm than the original sin.

Once a name is attached to the sin, a remedy can be presented. Remember that this type of failure we are discussing is the manifestation of sin in a person's life. **A specific sin cannot be forgiven, purged, or**

**cleansed if it is not known.** Honesty requires confession. Confession can be equated to a cleansing agent. Consider this analogy: if a child falls off

 *The prevailing attitude of the ministering leader must contain absolutely no judgment...*

his bike and scrapes his knee, the first action of the parent is to clean the abrasion. This removes the dirt, as well as any germ-laden particles that have the potential to cause infection and inflammation. They will then apply an antibacterial ointment to rid the body of dangerous bacteria. Confession can therefore be likened to the cleaning of a wound followed by the application of ointment that draws the bacteria of sin to the surface. Cleaning an abrasion or confessing sin can be both excruciating and humbling for the individual submitting to this cleansing process.

Confession should also follow a specific chain of order. For example, after my own failure, I first confessed my sin to God, and only then to my family. Following this, I confessed it to the body of Christ, and then publicly, to those in the community to whom I was connected. **The leader must assist the broken in this process.** Their confession must be honest and precise and must first be made to God. As they confess, their action opens the door to God's forgiveness in their life.

Scripture explains the necessity of confession:

*"He that covereth his sins shall not prosper: but whoso confesseth and forsaketh them shall have mercy."* – Proverbs 28:13 (KJV)

A private sin does not require a major public confession, but it still requires a confession to God and to those it has adversely affected. As a general rule, confession should be shared with those who have been directly affected by the sin. The leader must use Godly wisdom and discernment in this process. As Scripture promises, when one confesses, they shall have mercy. Mercy is the gift from God that every leader must demonstrate while attending to each one who confesses. If you push for a confession with the wrong motive, it can backfire. On the other hand,

>  ...confession should be shared with those who have been directly affected by the sin.

if you do not make it a requirement, then the process of restoration can never take place.

### STEP TWO – REPENTANCE

Confession and repentance may be thought of as two easy steps – a basic process that any Christian leader would know to begin with. However, what cannot be stressed enough is the importance of the leader's motive in this process. The leader's agenda must be founded on a pure desire to help, and must also be genuine in its goal of restoration for the individual who has fallen. If the leader has any other agenda not guided by love and mercy, they will do more damage than good. **The leader must see the fallen individual as a broken vessel and himself as God's instrument.** In this, the leader is able to fulfill the role of the Potter's wheel, allowing God to reshape the marred vessel. It requires the leader to take 'self' out of the picture and to hear everything that is said with God's ears, and to respond with God's heart. As the leader does their part, they open the door for the Holy Spirit to operate, enabling God to accomplish His plan for that individual.

Remorse is not the same as repentance. Remorse is a feeling, whereas repentance is an action. Repentance is the door one walks through after the confession. It is driven by a desire to change. This is what repentance represents: a turning away from a specific sin. When an individual confesses their sin and receives God's forgiveness, they must then confirm this step through the action of turning away from whatever brought them to this place. Repentance is not just an experience at the altar. In many of our churches, we call the sinner to the altar and have them confess to God and then verbally repent. As soon as they are done, we push to move them through the salvation process or claim they have been delivered, saved, or born again. Yet, when this individual walks out that church door, they have only just begun the repentance process.

They must now put into immediate action a change of course for their life.

To demonstrate a repentant nature requires action. It may mean one has to end certain relationships, find new places to socialize, or perhaps even to seek a new place of employment. Radical changes must take place to eliminate the possibility of backsliding – a term used in in Christendom for those who relapse into their old ways. During this process of repentance, the leader must be readily available to pray with the fallen individual, to guide them through any potential difficulties, to instruct them in Biblical truths, and to correct them whenever necessary. By devising systems of accountability, the leader puts in place

> " Radical changes must take place to eliminate the possibility of backsliding.

guard posts for the broken. The bottom line is that the leader is needed to nurse that individual through this process, because repentance is a journey that will take time.

### STEP THREE – MAKING AMENDS

In order to move the repentant individual forward there is a need for closure, but this is only possible when a genuine attempt is made to redress the original failure if possible. In certain situations, not everything can be rectified, because some sins and crimes have no adequate form of restitution. The leader must stress the reality of what can and cannot be done, reminding the individual that all sins are forgiven, whether they have been able to make full restitution or not.

Certain situations, especially those that have had a negative impact on others, will require a formal apology. Based on the circumstances, the leader may be needed to facilitate such a step. The leader will need to assess the situation; find a neutral place, and become the facilitator of the apology. Not every individual who has been hurt is ready or willing to accept an apology. This is where the practical wisdom of a leader is critical in addressing this point. By helping the broken to walk through the process, while preventing the repentant individual from unnecessary abuse at the hands of those he or she is apologizing to, the role of leadership is that of arbitrator and intercessor.

Then there are cases where some form of restitution is necessary in

> " Not every individual who has been hurt is ready or willing to accept an apology.

addition to an apology. In my situation, I apologized for my actions and agreed to pay more than forty thousand dollars – as requested – in an attempt to make things right. Restitution is not a foreign concept in the Bible and can be seen both in the Old and New Testaments. The Israelites in the Old Testament were under the law and therefore bound by specific requirements when it came to restitution. The Book of Exodus spells out the process of restitution for a variety of situations occurring in those times:

> "If a man shall steal an ox, or a sheep, and kill it, or sell it; he shall restore five oxen for an ox, and four sheep for a sheep. 2 If a thief be found breaking up, (this means the thief is caught at

night) and be smitten that he die, there shall no blood be shed for him. 3 If the sun be risen upon him, there shall be blood shed for him; for he should make full restitution; if he have nothing, then he shall be sold for his theft. 4 If the theft be certainly found in his hand alive, whether it be ox, or ass, or sheep; he shall restore double. 5 If a man shall cause a field or vineyard to be eaten, and shall put in his beast, and shall feed in another man's field; of the best of his own field, and of the best of his own vineyard, shall he make restitution. 6 If fire break out, and catch in thorns, so that the stacks of corn, or the standing corn, or the field, be consumed therewith; he that kindled the fire shall surely make restitution."
– Exodus 22:1-6 (KJV) (Explanation added in brackets above)

Leviticus is another Biblical book in which restitution is addressed. It identifies situations where stolen property was to be restored, along with the requirement for an additional one fifth of the value of the property to be returned.[218] What is also noteworthy from this passage is that the requirement of the restitution included making amends both with the offended and with God.[219] The leader must help the broken to recognize that their failure has not only affected those they hurt, but it has also offended God.

One final Biblical representation I wish to share concerning this step relates to Jesus visiting the house of Zacchaeus, a chief tax collector. When Jesus entered the home of Zacchaeus, the crowd which had gathered outside started talking about Jesus. They were confused about

> The leader must help the broken to recognize that their failure...has also offended God.

Jesus associating Himself with this chief publican, who was known to be oppressive and deceitful in his dealings. But during Jesus' visit, Zacchaeus was convicted of his sin, which led him to make the following proclamation:

*"Behold, Lord, the half of my goods I give to the poor; and if I have taken any thing from any man by false accusation, I restore him fourfold."* – Luke 19:8 (KJV)

As a result of Zacchaeus confessing his sins, showing remorse for his actions, and committing to making restitution for his wrongs, Jesus responded in this fashion:

*"This day is salvation come to this house, forsomuch as he also is a son of Abraham.* 10

*"For the Son of man is come to seek and to save that which was lost."* – Luke 19:9-10 (KJV)

**As a result of the actions taken by Zacchaeus, Jesus immediately instituted restoration into his life.** It was the result of Zacchaeus being honest about his past, confessing his sins, and committing to making things right by giving back what he had taken, along with an additional punitive offering that induced Jesus' proclamation. This narrative demonstrates the first three foundational steps necessary for restoration and instructively guides the broken through this process. When this process is followed, God Himself will open the doors of heaven and bring forth a restorative spirit that no man can hinder.

The church cannot be selective in its giving of mercy and grace, but should rather be inclusive and humble as it reaches out to assist all who have fallen. Proverbs 24:16 reminds us that a just man can fall seven times and rise up again. Only God can be the judge of one's soul. The leader must be the vessel that God uses to aid those who have messed up. Even when they have messed up more than once, if they are willing to submit to the process yet again, it is the leader's duty to bring them back to that place God has ordained for their life.

 The leader must be the vessel that God uses to aid those who have messed up.

**STEP FOUR – BIBLICAL DISCIPLINE**

This step is a transitional phase in that the requirements now lay heavily on the guidance of the leader and not the broken individual. This step requires the leader, through the church body, to develop a disciplinary process for the individual seeking restoration. **Discipline must meet the standards of the failure.** As a caution, be very careful to ensure that no preferential treatment is extended to any individual over another. Even though each process may differ – based on the specific sin involved, as well as the surrounding circumstances – each process must still be rooted in Biblical principles. The basic boundaries for discipline may include the following:

- **Counsel and Reflection:** The leader works with the individual in rebuilding his or her relationship with God. This is necessary to the process, as sin separates people from God, hence their broken state. This may involve instructing the individual in assigned reading materials; scheduled times of joint prayer and fasting; ministering and counseling through their emotional ups and downs; and addressing practical matters relating to the consequences of their broken state.
- **Regular Accountability Meetings:** This platform enables the broken individual to meet with a leader or ministry team to share the ongoing steps in their restoration process. They are encouraged to speak about their struggles and accomplishments, thereby creating

opportunities to hold themselves accountable. Within these appointed times, advice, counsel, and prayer are offered where necessary by leadership.

- **Restitution and Amends:** Leadership documents the commitment to make amends through apologies and restitution. The leadership team guides the individual to fulfill these mandates, and receives regular reports updating them on progress made or the difficulties encountered.

- **Goals and Objectives:** A game plan must be developed that focuses on the restoration process. The objectives should focus on the steps needed to bring the individual into a rightful relationship with God. The goal is to focus on the individual's walk with God, in specific relation to their perceived function within the body of Christ. Although discussions may be introduced by the broken individual about their position or status, this is not the primary focus here. The broken individual should rather focus on their renewed position or status in Christ. No guarantees should ever be made regarding the position or status of an individual , especially pertaining to a specific outcome for following the required steps.

This work requires a commitment by the leader to hang in, despite the difficulties encountered, never wavering, nor becoming weary of the process. Shortcuts and a lack of consistency on the part of leadership will sabotage the work of the Holy Spirit in the life of the broken vessel.

Remember, Paul's epistle to the Galatians[220] opens with a warning to the mature leader that this work of restoration must be done with all humility, while taking note of 'self' by carefully considering your own intention throughout the process. If not done in this manner, a leader may find him or her self tempted by any number of faults. Discipline in this

> Shortcuts and a lack of consistency on the part of leadership will sabotage the work...

process should never be driven by a punitive or judgmental nature, but should rather be built upon a foundation of forgiveness and redemption.

## STEP FIVE – RESTORATION

When this step is reached, the fruits of an individual's labor will be manifested. Honesty and transparency will have been demonstrated through confession; repentance will have been demonstrated by a change in values and lifestyle; making amends through apologies and/or restitution will have been sought and fulfilled wherever possible; and Biblical discipline will have been followed with integrity... it is at this point, when all of the aforementioned steps have been worked through and attained, that recognition of such change should be acknowledged by leadership and from within the church body.

As God continues to transform the individual's life, those who have worked with the person through this process can then celebrate the redemptive and restorative work done through Christ. At this stage, the individual will know that some doors may be permanently closed, while other doors may have the potential to be opened at a future date. They will already have experienced, or will currently be experiencing, the reopening of old doors, while new doors will also be opened for them as a result of their currently improved state of being. **In all, give God glory for a fallen soldier who has been restored before all of heaven.** Remember too that particular promise of a place with Christ, which has once again become obtainable to those experiencing restoration.

In concluding this chapter, it must be emphasized that there are no two circumstances alike. As a leader, you might be surprised by those who come before you in a state of brokenness. You may be even more surprised by the offenses that brought them to this place. Regardless of the individual's title, status, or influence, the Word of God has guidelines for restoration that are not only valid but necessary to attaining that specific goal. Many of God's broken vessels can be restored to a place of service in heaven's army. This can be achieved by following the relevant Biblical steps, recognizing the appropriate timing of specific steps within the overall process, and enabling a heaven-guided spirit to be encouraged back into righteousness. Just as the prodigal son in Luke[221] was welcomed back home and restored to his rightful place, so can the broken vessel be restored to the place and purpose for which he was originally created in Christ.

> Many of God's broken vessels can be restored to a place of service in heaven's army.

## Your Thoughts...

# Chapter Fourteen
## Personal Transformation[222]

*"Transformation does not start with some one else changing you; transformation is an inner self reworking of what you are now to what you will be."*
— **Byron Pulsifer**[223]

God allows in His wisdom what He can easily prevent by His power.[224] **God is still in control; no matter what you think is happening.** Sin and failure are a part of our lives, and returning from failure through God's grace is part of what makes us overcomers. Failure, and the resultant brokenness, can be used by God to refine our characters into becoming what He wants us to be for the work He has planned for us.

We see this in the life of Joseph – In Psalm 105[225] the psalmist had this insight into Joseph's life: God was not about to give an inexperienced youngster a significant anointing without some major internal changes.

Joseph was "humbled, greatly humbled."[226] He arrived in Egypt as a slave in iron chains, with his soul entered into the iron, and was tried and tested by the word of the Lord.[227] Then he was falsely accused of a heinous crime which "did in a special manner grieve him, and went to his heart; yet all this was the way to his preferment"[228] (advancement). Joseph trusted God's word to come to pass, even when his faith and patience were tested to the extreme, so that "though it linger," it "speaks of the end and will not prove false," and that His word would certainly come to pass at the appointed time.[229]

Then at the allotted time, after being thirteen years in Egypt, when Joseph was ready for the work God had outlined for him, God elevated him to become ruler over Egypt, second only to Pharaoh. If you want to be one of those people who are sent to be involved in a great work of God, you must be prepared to be tested (proved true NIV),[230] and be aware there is a price to pay. As God shapes and molds you, He will

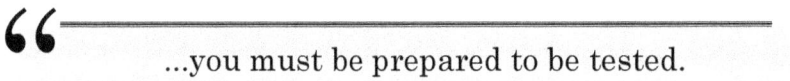

> ...you must be prepared to be tested.

allow - or has already allowed - your imperfections and your failures to be brought to the surface. He cannot bring you to the place He has ordained for your life until such issues are addressed. Even though your rebellion that resulted in sin, God has already established a road to your restoration. Just as God worked through Joseph, using his innocence to gain the favor of the other people, He knows your strengths too, and has already put a process in place to restore you.

Joseph was a true man of God because he understood the ways of God – he understood process. Joseph understood that in order to move any individual from one realm of the spirit to another (more enlightened) realm of the spirit, God uses a specific process, a series of steps that takes the individual to that place God wants them to be.[231] In His wisdom, God enables us to go through this transformation process by allowing us to experience a crisis in our lives. So don't be dismayed when you do experience crises in your life, as these moments in time are given to us to initiate the process of transformation God has planned for us. This is not to say that God has created the crisis – we do well enough on our own when it comes to instigating crises in our lives. God simply recognizes that He can use your current circumstances to promote you to a new spiritual understanding of the ultimate success encapsulated within failure. God uses crisis to open up a process in which a series of steps unfolds to take us out of our current distress into a place of God's development.[232]

I'm sure Joseph must have been utterly distraught when he was first sold into slavery by his brothers, but as the process of his crisis began to unfold, he clung to the promises of God that he had been taught. He began to understand that the transformation process he was experiencing was merely a series of steps taking him to where God could best use him for His divine purpose. Joseph recognized that God was in control.[233] This recognition made it easier for Joseph to submit to the process of

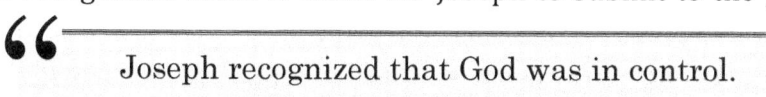

> Joseph recognized that God was in control.

personal transformation, for he was able to grasp the fact that he could be more effective for God when he was carried through this process within the will of God. His own journey taught him that as long as God was in control of his life and his destiny, he would always be a useful agent to God, irrespective of where he was placed in God's plan.

A time of crisis that initiates a transformative process usually begins with a declaration of God's intent for the life of the individual who is about to move through this process. These declarations of God's intent for our lives can come through vision, calling, or prophecy.[234] **Times of crisis are normally followed by a season of distress.** This hardship is experienced when God begins to grapple with who you are, to bring about in you the necessary and indispensable change to turn you from who you are now into the person He wants you to be.

Remember Jacob's struggle with the angel of the Lord on the banks of the Jabbok River?[235] That particular grappling session transformed Jacob, whose name meant "deceiver,"[236] into the man who became "Israel." Isra-El, can mean *"He who prevails with God,"* or *"May God prevail,"* depending on the context.[237]

We know that Jacob was very distressed prior to his wrestling match with the angel, so much so that he sent his family across the Jabbok River first, so he could deal more appropriately with the process of transformation he was experiencing.[238] Similarly, Joseph also experienced distress. The interesting part about their distress is that because of it, both men underwent radical development. This is simply a part of the process. God was dealing with specific issues of character within both of these men, but He was simultaneously also developing a new strength of character within each of them. **The development of a strengthened character is often accompanied by bouts of high-level distress.**[239] Joseph's brothers visibly saw the level of his distress, or "the anguish of his soul."[240] On the part of Jacob, who was in the process of becoming Israel, God chose to use his distress as a method of showing him how repulsive was the accumulated sin in his life. Jacob was no good to God as a "deceiver." God needed a man who could stand his ground in the fullness of his integrity. Joseph was perhaps too arrogant, being his father's favorite. He possibly needed a lesson in humility. In both these cases, their moments of human distress were in essence an accumulation of God's dissatisfaction with vessels who were not achieving their full potential.

In my own personal failure, my issues were pride and deceit. God

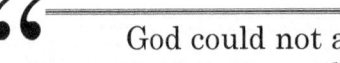

> God could not and will not us a prideful deceiver.

could not and will not use a prideful deceiver . It may have worked well for the devil and it at times gave me brief moments of satisfaction, but it certainly was not what God ever intended for my life (and as for the devil, his days are numbered!). My personal decisions brought me to that place, and in turn, God had to intervene with a crisis of epic proportion to grab my attention. It was this distress that pointed me back to the cross and back to God's grace and mercy, of which I was totally underserving.

And as is evident with most human distress, it has the potential to lead to transformation. God wants to use us to perform His will at the level of our highest capability. Often, within our own personal transformation, God shows us what we are like without Jesus, but He never shows us

> God wants to use us to perform His will at the level of our highest capability.

how ugly we are without also showing us how beautiful His grace is.[241]

We aren't given too many details concerning the decision Joseph's brothers made to sell him into slavery, but we can assume he had become insufferably proud. Given the dreams he had, pride is perhaps understandable, but not excusable. Without God intervening to yank out that pride, replacing it with humility, Joseph would no doubt have remained a cracked vessel out of which his vital potential would slowly have leaked away. Who can tell what would have happened to Jacob had he not chosen to face the weakness of deception within himself that night on the banks of the Jabbok?

Perhaps his brother, Esau, would not have been so welcoming. **People sense weakness in others, as much as they recognize those who exude strength.** In His wisdom, God allows what He can easily prevent by His power.[242] In the trauma of your circumstances, understand that God is developing your strengths. He is in the process of turning your potential into something actual and real. Rest assured that when the process of your development has reached a certain point of God's choosing, what follows is the demonstration of all that God said to you in the very beginning.[243]

Joseph had two prophetic dreams in the Book of Genesis[244] – both dreams declared God's will and power over Joseph's life, and through his life to others. His brothers hated him for his dreams; even his father rebuked him, though his father recognized the interpretation. His brothers were jealous of him, *"but his father observed the saying."*[245] No one questioned the interpretation; they just didn't like the person God was going to use. This jealousy frequently occurs in the Kingdom. People will allow others their place, as long as it's not bigger than their own. [246]

> People will allow others their place, as long as it's not bigger than their own.

These visions were all about ruling and reigning, and Joseph had to be prepared for that. Joseph spoke freely about his calling, given to him through his dreams, but felt a deep "*anguish*" in "*his soul*"[247] when the time arrived for his training. Yet he desperately needed training! He needed development, and he needed exposure to authority. God had to make Joseph fit the vision he had been given. In prophecy there is often an apparent contradiction. The contradiction is the journey from revelation to manifestation – the journey from prophecy spoken to prophecy revealed and fulfilled.[248] We see this in the lives of many Bible characters. It took about twenty-two years for David to become the king of Israel after the prophet Samuel revealed his destiny to him. Joseph is another case in point.

When significant prophecy has come into people's lives, often – not always, as it depends on what God has to do in them – people's lives go in a different direction. This happens because once your calling or destiny has been revealed, **God will focus on the first thing in you that will stop your calling from taking place**.[249] Perhaps the reason Joseph had to lose the status of favored son was because this mindset would have hindered his calling through a lack of humility. God has to lift our character and integrity to the same level as our word of destiny, and only when our character meets the level of our destiny can our calling begin to be actualized in the physical world. Sometimes God allows you to go down before He raises you up to the new level He requires of you.

When Samuel anointed David to be King, I bet the young shepherd boy thought of living in the royal palace, wearing fine clothes and having servants in waiting. He had no idea that it would take two decades of preparation, that he would lose his best friend, be chased mercilessly by his present king and have to hide in the wilderness. His life seemed to be in direct contrast to his anointing. Apart from the band of rebels who joined him, everyone seemed to be against him. He had to teach his band of rebels to stand together and fight as a unit. David had to earn their respect and loyalty. He had to learn to trust God for food and all the other necessary requirements for life while being hunted and living in caves. To become a man after God's own heart he had to be trained and

> To become a man after God's own heart he had to be trained and equipped by God,

equipped by God, as well as having to endure those unsuitable elements of his character being dealt with by God.

Part of the equipping is learning to take rejection. Joseph was rejected and sold off by his brothers. The physical agony of slavery is incomparable to the anguish of betrayal. To walk in Jesus' footsteps you need to accept that He was rejected by men and familiar with sorrow and heartache. Men of God frequently have to spend time alone with God, where they are forced to choose between bitterness and self-improvement. An important part of this process includes learning to trust God in all things, while making a conscious decision not to reject those people who have hurt us. We have to give ourselves up to the process of God. To earn the anointing to govern a country, Joseph needed to undergo his own trial. Ultimately everyone must be restored from all their rejections and hurts. Joseph turned away from his brothers and wept after meeting them again.[250] He understood that it was God who directed him to Egypt, and no one else. He could not hold the rejection against them, as it was part of God's plan for his character forging.[251] Bitterness and unforgivingness towards those who rejected you will obstruct the path to restoration. We need to always remember that God is in control and that He works for the good of those who love Him.[252]

Jesus before the cross; innocent, a Jew rejected by Jews, handed over by a friend to be whipped, beaten and disgraced, He says: *"Now is my soul troubled..."*[253] He didn't ask His Father to save Him, instead, accepting the purpose for which He had been sent He chose obedience, saying, *"Father, glorify Thy name."*[254] In profound pain and suffering, this can be our only reaction.

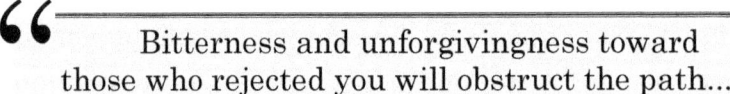

> Bitterness and unforgivingness toward those who rejected you will obstruct the path…

Joseph came to a place where he realized his brothers were simply instruments that were used to set in motion God's detailed plan for Joseph's life. Joseph's acceptance that God intended his personal crisis for his own good, as well as that of two nations (Israel and Egypt), is a good reflection of his healed character. **Pain and discomfort are needed if we are going to reflect the image of Jesus.** He was despised and rejected of men, a man of sorrows and acquainted with grief.[255] Healing is essential after our trials and rejection because when we are hurt and crushed by people we tend to have an ungodly response. We are apt to vow never to trust people again, resolving to never again become too emotionally attached to others. These concealed hurts inhibit us from living through the richness of God in worship; they prevent us from achieving breakthroughs in our lives. This gives Satan so much to work with and use against us. While we cling to our pain, we allow the devil space to operate in these areas of our lives, where he can neutralize us as he pleases.

It is essential that you see your past in view of God's dealings with you in the present, and that you reach a place of giving thanks. Scripture says, *"In every thing give thanks: for this is the will of God in Christ Jesus concerning you."*[256] When you look back and recognize God's work in the way people treated you, the healing process becomes easier and happens more quickly. This is worth bearing in mind for future reference concerning those occasions where you might again be hurt. God was doing a work in Joseph that would give him the ability to rule over Pharaoh's leading men. You cannot rule over anything unless you

 You cannot rule over anything unless you first learn to rule over your own heart.

first learn to rule over your own heart. [257] Those people who are in tune with the will of God will be accessible for Him to use in the process of spiritual warfare. Their ability to tap in to the Holy Spirit allows them to understand specifically what God wants to do. If you have experienced failure, the difficulties you may be going through could very well be related to your spiritual progress. The work God is doing in you is often equated to the work he wants to do through you. The hardship you might currently be experiencing will probably become a powerful testimony for others who will be set free by your life message. This is one of many good reasons God allows us to fail in the first place – to form a unique experiential wisdom within each individual that can easily be shared with utter conviction.

This is precisely what happened to Joseph. What he learned during his difficult days in the house of Potiphar became of great use to him when he was finally elevated to the position of Pharaoh's right-hand man. The testing of his purity while he was a slave in Potiphar's house taught him that maintaining his integrity in the face of adversity would serve God best, because in the end, the truth is always revealed, and will always set us free. When we make this connection, we can actually find pleasure while serving in a difficult environment, as we know that whatever serves God best serves us best too. **We need to understand that the skills we learn during times of hardship and adversity will benefit us in our future.** Even though you might currently think you are wasting time because you are not operating within your true calling, hindsight will often show you a very different picture. God uses hardship to teach us what He wants us to know.

Both David and Joseph serve as great examples of this practical truth. Scripture informs us of David's struggle between being anointed by Samuel and finally becoming king. Everything he learned during those two difficult decades gave him the strength and wisdom needed to rule Israel. Joseph, who had no direct promise of his anointing through a human agent, must have wondered at times why he had invested so much trust in those dreams he had as a youth. Even so, he never turned away from God. Joseph used the opportunities he was presented with while living in Egypt. He learned the agricultural system of Egypt, as well as their language and culture. He learned administration, finance, business, and people management.[258] What both Joseph and David learned in times of adversity stayed with them and formed the basis of their future. Within the trials both men suffered there was a testing of their purity.

Joseph refrained from succumbing to the seduction of Potiphar's wife. David refused to kill Saul on two different occasions,[259] who he still honored as God's anointed, in spite of being ruthlessly hunted by the king. Human trials are generally accompanied by a test. While both men passed these tests of purity, David later failed due to the impure nature of his thoughts, which led to unwise words in summoning Bathsheba, followed by the impure deed of adultery. While we yet breathe, we are

> While we yet breathe, we are constantly being tested and refined.

constantly being tested and refined. The good news is that even when we fail any of the tests thrown at us through the course of our daily lives, we are given the opportunity to take them again, and again, until we pass... the goodness of God will never fail you. He keeps giving you another chance until you succeed.[260]

When Joseph had been elevated to a place of authority in Potiphar's house, his virtue was attacked as a test on his purity. He did not fail this test because he was in communion with God, and therefore did not sin against God. His awareness of God was far stronger than the appeal of casual sex with Potiphar's wife.[261] God will never test us more than we

> God will never test us more than we can endure · our trials will be in proportion...

can endure[262] – our trials will be in proportion to our strength [263] – and each trial will be built upon the last. As those issues in our lives which need to be addressed are overcome, we are more prepared for God to tackle the next issue, and the next, until we reach that place where we are able to accomplish the work God has set before us. However, until the current trial has been overcome, until that specific work required in us is complete, we cannot move to the next level of elevation – ever closer to where God needs us to be. It may seem that each new test or trial is bigger than the last, but it needs to be. We don't learn from something we already know; we don't become stronger by fighting something weaker. You only climb higher by going uphill.

That's why we have the Holy Spirit. He comes alongside us, in us, and guides us. When we turn to Him He strengthens us, wanting us to succeed, wanting us to grow in Him so we can be used for the great works He has planned for us. He knows the plans He has for you, plans to prosper you and not to harm you, plans to give you hope and a future.[264]

Failure and the accompanying distress can be used by God to develop you, and to grow you into a vessel of honor. **Remember the words God is giving you over your life and hold onto them.** Don't be caught up in anger or bitterness towards the people who have judged or rejected you. Pray for them. Pray that they never make the mistakes you have made, and remember that what they did to you is part of your development and life message. You must realize that essentially, you are having to endure the distress you currently feel so that God, through these circumstances, can forge you into the man or woman you were created to be in Christ. The evidence or confirmation that God is working through you is the very fact that you are going through this time of distress. If you lose sight of the development process you are undergoing, you will become bitter and disillusioned. If disillusionment is pressing in on you, you should strive to get back on track with your development process and recognize what God is doing in you. God is faithful. He will never forsake you. God has things to say to you, and He has things to show you.

God wants to reveal Himself to you, and He will use this season of distress and development in your life to do so. Don't lose sight of the majesty and sovereignty of God by feeling sorry for yourself during this time. God doesn't measure time; He recognizes growth,[265] so the process

> God doesn't measure time; He recognizes growth.

or season doesn't need to be protracted. The key is co-operation with the Holy Spirit, as this ensures you need only be in this season for as long as the growth process requires you to be. Just seek God and be obedient to what He shows you. Note the presence of God in your situation; take notice of the subtle nuances of the Holy Spirit as He works in you, and the countless encouragements He gives you while you are going through this experience. **You are where God wants you to be so He can shape you into the vessel He needs you to be.** You won't need to speak from anyone else's notes; you will have your life message directly from God. We all need to die to rebellion and independence, so we might gain humility, and accountability to God. Only then will you begin to see the prophetic words God has pronounced over your life start taking shape and coming into being. It takes real submission to God for Him to thoroughly change you.

In your current crisis or situation, when things are going against you, you need to ask yourself: "What are the words that God has spoken over me? What's going on inside of me? What am I giving birth to in these circumstances? What work is God doing in me; what is so deep that it demands this kind of pain, sacrifice and difficulty? What is God doing in allowing by His wisdom what He could prevent by His power?"

## Your Thoughts...

# Chapter Fifteen
## Understand Why God Allowed you to Experience Failure[266]

*"My imperfections and failures are as much a blessing from God as my successes and my talents and I lay them both at his feet."*[267]
– **Mahatma Ghandi**

Why does God allow us to experience failure? Why did God give human beings free will, knowing all the while that they would exercise this free will, even if it was contrary to His supreme will? An omnipotent (all powerful) and omniscient (all-knowing) Creator who works outside of linear time surely knew all along that Adam and Eve would commit the sin of disobedience? Yes! God knew that Adam and Eve would choose sin over their right-relationship with Him. Well, if God knew that much, then He also knew He would have to send His son to die on a cross, so humanity could be redeemed. God accepted this exceptionally high price His son would have to pay. Jesus accepted the ignominy of crucifixion before the heavens and the earth were ever created! When God first molded Adam into His own form and breathed life into him, He did it in the knowledge that His son, Jesus, would die a horrible physical death as a result of redeeming this masterpiece of His creation, Adam. He knew too that billions of human beings would be born into a life of sinfulness because of the terrible choice made by Adam and Eve to acquire knowledge by their own means. And yet God chose to persevere with His plan of creation, knowing what would be unleashed on all of humanity and the rest of creation. Why did God allow sin to enter into

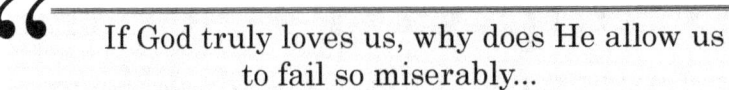
> If God truly loves us, why does He allow us to fail so miserably...

the world? If God truly loves us, why does He allow us to fail so miserably at certain times in our lives?

Let me put this another way. Imagine that every person who has ever lived (except for Jesus, who is both human and divine) was given the opportunity to live in the Garden of Eden as Adam and Eve lived before their fall. How long would it have taken each of these individuals before they too tried the fruit forbidden to them by God? Would any human being have managed to withstand the temptation of tapping in to an unknown source of knowledge – the knowledge of good and evil? For a time, perhaps, but ultimately, all of us would finally have chosen the path to knowledge! God knew that too. He is the source of all wisdom, and His wisdom is the source of all knowledge. The Book of Proverbs makes this clear: *"For the Lord giveth wisdom: out of his mouth cometh knowledge and understanding."*[268] Many other Scriptures confirm God as the source of wisdom.[269] **So, God in His absolute wisdom knew that humanity would disobey His direct command to gratify their thirst for knowledge.**

But here is the most important part of this scenario: God wanted us to have this knowledge! In the fullness of His appointed timing, we would surely have acquired the knowledge of good and evil. How else would we ever truly distinguish between good and evil? Why would God deliberately place this specific tree in the middle of Eden if its placement did not coincide with His will for humanity to eat thereof? His decree forbidding Adam and Eve to eat from the tree surely restricts the timing of how God wanted this knowledge revealed to them. But, if God had not included their potential fall in his master plan for humanity, He would surely have refrained altogether from placing this tree in Eden. Perhaps if Adam and Eve had refused to be deceived by the serpent, choosing rather to honor God's prohibition, their obedience might have been rewarded by that very act! They would have recognized evil for what it is, without having to gain experiential knowledge of it. I doubt God would have minded them questioning His decree, for He would then have been presented with an opportunity to reveal to them the serpent's devious scheme. But in choosing to disobey God, they exposed themselves to the full brunt of a limited earthly existence without the protective mantle of God's glory surrounding them. They had chosen to make themselves vulnerable to Satan's attack. They chose to experience the knowledge of evil that came through disobedience. Consider the notion that human beings would one day be admitted into the New Jerusalem without firsthand knowledge of how dangerous and destructive evil can be... Adam and Eve had already been given complete experiential knowledge of good, and while I am unable to reference this idea from Scripture, I can't help thinking that God always intended for us to gain

> I can't help thinking that God always intended for us to gain the knowledge...

the knowledge of both good and evil. We were simply too impatient to wait on God. We trusted the word of another over His benevolent instruction. Perhaps the most common downfall of human beings is that we prize self-gratification above obedience to God. We also lack God's patience. God knew from the start that we would have to learn the hard way. We would have to learn that free will encompasses the freedom to fail and the propensity to fall.

What about the fall of Lucifer, who became Satan after being thrown out of heaven? He was involved in the fall of Adam and Eve, and his story is therefore surely relevant to our own. In the Book of Ezekiel, we find passages that seem to be a particularly strong indictment against the king of Tyre, who lived in the prophet Ezekiel's day.[270] The king is rebuked for his insatiable pride and greed. The excerpt below puts into context the concept that the prophet Ezekiel is actually rendering a dual prophecy:

However, some of the descriptions in Ezekiel 28:11–19 go beyond any mere human king. In no sense could an earthly king claim to be "*in Eden*" or to be "*the anointed cherub who covers*" or to be "*on the holy mountain of God.*" Therefore, most Bible interpreters believe that Ezekiel 28:11–19 is a dual prophecy, comparing the pride of the king of Tyre to the pride of Satan. Some propose that the king of Tyre was actually possessed by Satan, making the link between the two even more powerful and applicable.[271]

What is particularly striking in the passage of Scripture referenced above, are the following two verses:

*"Thou wast perfect in thy ways from the day that thou wast created, till iniquity was found in thee.... Thine heart was lifted up because of thy beauty, thou hast corrupted thy wisdom by reason of thy brightness:...."* – Ezekiel 28:15 and Ezekiel 28:17 (KJV)

> Lucifer was created perfect in his ways, but he corrupted his wisdom...

Lucifer was created perfect in his ways, but he corrupted his wisdom by reason of his brightness. In other words, he began to convince himself that his beauty, rather than being a reflection of God's magnificence, was something unique for which he, Lucifer, ought to be credited. Consider the phrase: *"thou hast corrupted thy wisdom."* This tells us that when iniquity was found within him, he was already a wise being – he was already privy to the knowledge of good and evil. In spite of the knowledge and wisdom he had already acquired, he still chose to rebel against being a servant of God. It appears that when Lucifer and the rest of the angels were created, they had this information – the knowledge of good and evil – 'hardwired' into the essence of their being.

Consider this scenario: at some point in His omniscient musings, God realized that conscious beings who are given powerful information without earning it, or at least learning how to focus it, could use it for evil instead. When I say "at some point in His omniscient musings," I mean that in an all-knowing way, even before creating Lucifer, God knew he would rebel against His authority. Jesus Christ, the Son of God, is after all, identified as the *"Alpha and Omega, the beginning and the end, the first and the last."*[272] Lucifer allowed himself to be blinded to the holiness of God's love because he chose to focus too much of his attention on God's majesty, to the point where he craved that majesty for himself. In his attempt to usurp the God who created him, Lucifer fell to the earth

> In his attempt to usurp the God who created him, Lucifer fell to the earth...

like a bolt of lightning. [273] We know through Scripture that the first war ever to be waged took place in the heavens,[274] and that essentially we are still involved in that very same war today.[275] Knowing that Lucifer was corrupt and dwelling on the earth, God placed Adam and Eve in Eden, putting everything they saw at their disposal, but with one simple instruction: Do not eat the fruit of the tree in the middle of the garden.[276] And then God waited until the quest for humanity's knowledge of good and evil was initiated.

Adam and Eve gained through their failure the knowledge that choosing disobedience over obedience was detrimental to them and everything they loved. Unlike Adam and Eve, Lucifer chose disobedience even though he had the knowledge of good and evil instilled within him. His was a choice for evil in the full knowledge of what his choice would entail if he failed. It was an outright challenge to God, for which he could not be forgiven. Adam and Eve, however, were innocent of understanding the knowledge for which they thirsted. Recently retired from preaching, Robert L. Deffinbaugh,[277] serving full-time at bible.org, states this fact very clearly:

> Adam and Eve did not understand what "good" and "evil" were, nor did they really grasp what life or death were. These were all beyond their experience. They would have to trust God, His definitions, His distinctions, and His prohibitions.[278]

God forgave them because they did not fully comprehend the ramifications of their choice. He did not turn away from them, knowing that Satan had influenced them in their decision. What Satan did not understand is that, in a sense, he had fulfilled God's divine purpose in setting humanity on the path that would finally climax in the ushering in of the New Jerusalem.[279] This is the point I want you to understand: **even though Lucifer rebelled so he would no longer have to be a servant of God, he is still unable to operate independently from God**. Which means he is still serving God's ultimate purposes on the earth.[280] This concept is well documented in Christian literature. Erwin W. Lutzer's book, *The Serpent of Paradise: The Incredible Story of How Satan's Rebellion Serves God's Purposes,*[281] is just one example. Scripture also makes it clear that Satan cannot make a move without God's express consent. The legion of demons who were cast out by Jesus is a good example – they had to ask permission to enter a herd of swine.[282] In the words of Martin Luther, "Even the devil is God's devil."[283] No matter what nefarious activities Satan and his cohorts are up to on the earth, God is aware of their Machiavellian schemes, and has been working behind the scenes to create a positive outcome, for the good of those who love Him.

This is good to know, and interesting, but it still doesn't answer the initial question: Why does God allow us to experience failure?

God allows us to experience failure because human beings very

> God allows us to experience failure because human beings very seldon learn life lessons...

seldom learn life lessons by observing the mistakes of other people. We learn best when we experience things firsthand. If we were inclined to learn from the mistakes of others, Adam's failure to obey God would have been sufficient in serving as a lesson for those who followed. Consider Adam and Eve after they ate the forbidden fruit. Scripture tells us that Adam heard God's voice and he became afraid because he was naked, so he hid himself from God.[284] The Book of Proverbs informs us that: *"The fear of the Lord is the beginning of wisdom: and the knowledge of the holy is understanding."*[285] In Adam's very first encounter with God after disobeying His one direct command, he begins to act on the knowledge he has gained. For the first time in his life, Adam feared the Lord. Prior to this, he had been an innocent creature, bathed in God's love and generosity.

The verse describing Adam and Eve's birth into the realm of sin is very specific in its wording. We are told that their eyes *"were opened."*[286] Just like newborn babies, they could suddenly see themselves and the world around them with new eyes – eyes no longer bathed in the comfort of their spiritual amniotic fluid, but exposed instead to the harsh realities of their new carnal nature. In the time it took them to eat a piece of fruit, they suddenly perceived themselves differently, and the world around them had changed. Why is it that in the blink of an eye, they became ashamed of their nakedness? How is it that their nakedness was suddenly made apparent to them?

We are given an important clue in Psalm 8, which depicts why God is mindful of humankind: *"For thou hast made him a little lower than the angels, and hast crowned him with glory and honour"*[287] (emphasis added). Note that the Amplified Bible uses, "God [or heavenly beings])" in the place of "angels" – "Yet You have made him but a little lower than

God [or heavenly beings], and You have crowned him with glory and honor."²⁸⁸

I prefer this interpretation presented by the Amplified version of the Bible, especially when viewed in light of Paul's letter to the Corinthian Church: *"Know ye not that we shall judge angels? how much more things that pertain to this life?"*²⁸⁹ (emphasis added). This passage makes it pretty clear that humans are placed below God but above the angels. Coming back to the point, when God created Adam and Eve a little lower than Himself, He crowned them with glory! Herein lies the answer to the question I posed earlier: the reason Adam and Eve's nakedness was suddenly made apparent to them is due to the fact that they lost the glory they had been crowned with prior to their sin of disobedience. The original Hebrew word for "crowned" in this sense is derived from the verb, `atar which means "to encircle," "to surround."²⁹⁰ Their sin

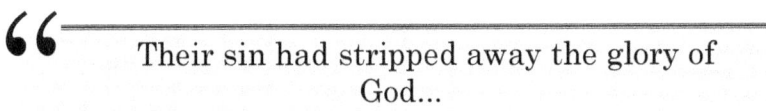

> Their sin had stripped away the glory of God...

had stripped away the glory of God which had surrounded them from the time God had first breathed life into them. Little wonder they were afraid!

While God clothed Adam and Eve with animal skins for their immediate comfort and to offer them a semblance of dignity, He also put into place the next phase of His master plan for humanity by promising to send a Savior for them.

In Paul's letter to the Galatians, he reminds them that in Christ Jesus we are all children of God through faith, for *"as many of you as have been baptized into Christ have put on Christ."*²⁹¹ The New International Version of the Bible puts it like this: *"for all of you who were baptized into Christ have clothed yourselves with Christ"*²⁹² (emphasis added). This reveals to us that those who accept Christ's Lordship over their lives are once more covered with the mantle of God's glory. Just as God immediately forgave Adam and Eve, choosing to clothe them and set them on a path to redemption through the seed of Eve, so is He looking to forgive all those

> ...He is looking to forgive all those who have failed.

who have failed. With great anticipation He waits to greet you with a kiss and a new robe of righteousness[293] so you will be properly dressed for the celebration of your homecoming.

It is only after his fall that Adam begins to recognize God's mercy, demonstrated by His response to Adam's sin, as well as Eve's. He and his wife had everything they needed before they sinned, given to them by God. But now that sin had entered Eden, God had to respond, for He could not allow sin to go unpunished. The manner in which God responded set the context for His glory to be revealed.

God knew all along that Lucifer would rebel against His authority, and deceive Eve, who would then lead Adam into choosing sin. God's master plan for the redemption of humanity, established before the foundation of the world, anticipated sin and the suffering it would bring.[294] In fact, God's plan was meticulously laid, making provision for sin through the preordained suffering of His own Son, Jesus.[295] The Acts of the Apostles, in reference to Jesus, make plain the fact that God knew all along His Son would have to suffer physical death at the hands of wicked men:

*"Him, being delivered **by the determinate counsel and foreknowledge of God**, ye have taken, and by wicked hands have crucified and slain: 24 Whom God hath raised up, having loosed the pains of death: because it was not possible that he should be holden of it." – Acts 2:23-24 (KJV) (Emphasis added)*

> Jesus would suffer the greatest ill-effect in order for humanity to acquire knowledge…

When we begin to understand this crucial fact, it is no longer possible to think of God as being harsh for allowing sin to enter the world. Jesus would suffer the greatest ill-effect in order for humanity to acquire the knowledge of good and evil![296] Adam and Eve's demand for immediate self-gratification created the need for their redemption, and that of their offspring. God's response to their sin is immediate, and encompassed within the curses placed on Adam, Eve, and Satan, are the means of humanity's eventual salvation.[297] Eve is told that "*in sorrow*" she will "*bring forth children*,"[298] yet in bearing children she has the ultimate victory over the serpent, for it is her seed who will crush the serpent's head.[299] The crushed head of the serpent, even though it bruises Christ's heel at Calvary, spells the beginning of the end of Satan's freedom to terrorize the earth.[300] The earth is cursed on Adam's behalf, and his labor is dramatically increased just to feed his family.[301] As a result he had to rely on God to provide him with good crops. Adam is also told he will experience physical death, and will return to the dust of the earth.[302] Adam's death sentence effectively provides the means of our salvation, because it is through Adam's lineage that Christ the Savior is born. Adam's death brings the assurance of eternal life for all who are born to the earth, through the life and death of the Lord Jesus Christ.[303]

With this understanding of God's detailed plan for humanity's redemption, we are given a glimpse of how God is able to turn a cosmic disaster into a successful process that leads to eternal life. **Now consider how much simpler it is for God to turn your private disaster into a successful process of restoration that leads to wisdom and greater faith in God.** Remember that God turned Adam and Eve out of the garden to prevent them from continuing to eat from the tree of life:

*"And the Lord God said, Behold, the man is become as one of us, to know good and evil: and now, lest he put forth his hand, and take also of the tree of life, and eat, and live for ever: 23 Therefore the Lord God sent him forth from the garden of Eden,..."* – Genesis 3:22 and partial rendering of Genesis 3:23 (KJV)

It stands to reason that Adam and Eve had already eaten fruit from the tree of life – it was never forbidden while they walked with God – but after they had sinned, their immortality was revoked by the curse

> " God in His absolute mercy, paved the path to their redemption...

of death. If they had eaten from the tree of life in their fallen state, they would have become like Lucifer: immortal beings with a nature that had become inherently evil, due to the choice they made in favor of sin. God, in His absolute mercy, paved the path to their redemption through the grace offered in Jesus Christ. We are also given assurance that the curse humanity still suffers will be removed when the servants of God are restored to eternal life. This aspect of God's master plan is made patently clear in the Revelation of Jesus Christ to John on the Isle of Patmos, where He reveals that it has always been God's plan to have human beings eat from the tree of life:

*"And he shewed me a pure river of water of life, clear as crystal, proceeding out of the throne of God and of the Lamb. 2 In the midst of the street of it, and on either side of the river, was there the tree of life, which bare twelve manner of fruits, and yielded her fruit every month: and the leaves of the tree were for the healing of the nations. 3 And there shall be no more curse: but the throne of God*

*and of the Lamb shall be in it; and his servants shall serve him: 4 And they shall see his face; and his name shall be in their foreheads."*
– Revelation 22:1-4 (KJV)

Adam's sin, and the curse which bound humanity into sinfulness, when factored into God's intricate plan of redemption, ultimately provide humanity with superior blessings to those lost by Adam's sin and the curse.[304] When Eve chose to disbelieve the word of God, choosing rather to believe the word of the serpent, she set a precedent for all of humanity. So God *"concluded them all in unbelief, that he might have mercy upon all."*[305] Essentially, sin was the starting point of humanity's

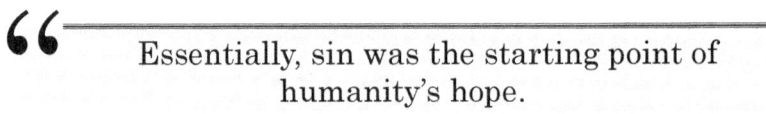

> Essentially, sin was the starting point of humanity's hope.

hope .[306] If you have experienced, or are still experiencing private or public failure as a result of sin, within the seed of your failure lies the starting point of your hope. Your sin provides the occasion for God's grace, bringing repentance, and reconciliation, which in turn leads to a more intimate union with God.[307] These are the reasons for God allowing us to experience failure.

As was established in chapter twelve, failure can be the result of sin, or it can simply be a practical life lesson we must endure to strengthen us in that particular area. Most billionaires and millionaires experience a string of business failures before finding a winning formula. Richard Branson is one such entrepreneur who tasted the bitterness of failure many times before becoming established as a successful businessman. While experiencing grave cash-flow problems, Richard involved himself in a tax evasion escapade relating to his Virgin record shops. He spent a night in prison, and paid £60,000 after his plea-bargain was accepted,[308] which at today's currency exchange rate is in the region of $92,184.00! Branson used this lesson to his advantage, making a quality choice to maintain his business integrity in all future dealings:

*"I vowed to myself that I would never again do anything that would cause me to be imprisoned or, indeed, do any kind of business deal that would embarrass me."*[309]

Even so, many of his business ventures failed along his path to success. Virgin Cola, Virgin Vodka, Virgin Vie, Virgin Brides, Virgin Clothing, Virgin Cars, and Virgin Digital all failed.[310] The lesson he shares is simple: "Learn from failure."[311] Failure should be treated as a golden opportunity

> Failure should be treated as a golden opportunity to acquire statistical feedback.

to acquire statistical feedback. In the spiritual realm, however, when sin leads to failure, the predicament you find yourself in can be God's way of seeking your attention.

Through our failures we are humbled, disciplined, and brought back into the fold of Christ. Not only does God refine us in our suffering, but He graciously explains His reasoning through Scripture:

*"Behold, I have refined thee, but not with silver; I have chosen thee in the furnace of affliction. 11 For mine own sake, even for mine own sake, will I do it: for how should my name be polluted? and I will not give my glory unto another."* – Isaiah 48:10-11 (KJV)

This passage of Scripture goes a long way toward explaining why God allows us to experience failure. **We are refined in the furnace of affliction for God's own sake.** Failure can be seen as a means of ridding us of our impurities so that we do not pollute God's name by association. He perseveres with us, knowing we will eventually bring glory to His name through our process of refinement. He refuses to give up on us, knowing that only Satan and his principalities will benefit from us becoming lost to Christ in the mire of our sins.

Consider the man who was born blind. He received his sight after Jesus had made a paste of mud and saliva, applying it to his eyes and commanding him to wash it off in the pool of Siloam.[312] His disciples asked whether it was him or his parents who had sinned, resulting in the man's blindness.[313] The answer Jesus gave to them gives us further insight into human suffering: "Jesus answered, *Neither hath this man sinned, nor his parents: but that the works of God should be made manifest in him.*"[314] Reading the entire passage, it becomes evident that this man's suffering eventually leads him to believe in the Son of God, and to worship Him.[315] This man's suffering is inconsequential when viewed in the light of eternity. His suffering brought about the process of his salvation.

> " His suffering brought about the process of his salvation.

However, for those Pharisees who cast the man out for insisting that Jesus was of God,[316] their suffering would be eternal… unless they came to the realization that Jesus Christ is the Lord of glory who deserves their honor, praise, and worship. The blind man's suffering – to this very day – still glorifies the works of God being made manifest in the lives of those who come to this realization through reading his story. Author, Randy Alcorn, in his book, *If God Is Good,*[317] enlightens our understanding by succinctly summing up in one paragraph the many reasons why God allows us to experience failure:

> *God uses suffering to purge sin from our lives, strengthen our commitment to him, force us to depend on his grace, bind us together with other believers, produce discernment, foster sensitivity, discipline our minds, impart wisdom, stretch our hope, cause us to know Christ better, make us long for truth, lead us to repentance of*

*sin, teach us to give thanks in times of sorrow, increase our faith, and strengthen our character. And once he accomplishes such great things, often we can see that our suffering has been worth it. God doesn't simply want us to feel good. He wants us to be good. And very often the road to being good involves not feeling good.*[318]

In closing this chapter, I would like to leave you with a powerful Scripture to meditate on, especially when struggling to understand a period of failure in your life, but also as a general 'rule of thumb' to guide you in your daily life:

*"Trust in the Lord with all thine heart; and lean not unto thine own understanding. 6 In all thy ways acknowledge him, and he shall direct thy paths."* – Proverbs 3:5-6 (KJV)

Broken

# Chapter Sixteen
## Understanding How Sharing Your Failure Fits God's Plan For Your Life[319]

*"Return to thine own house, and shew how great things God hath done unto thee. And he went his way, and published throughout the whole city how great things Jesus had done unto him."*
– Luke 8:39 (KJV)

After walking the path to restoration, I received an invitation to minister at a conference, and I was so thankful and grateful that God had brought me back to this place. Up to this point, I felt no desire to be in the 'public' eye. I had purposely stayed away from public events and was no longer connected to the processes and people that usually opened such doors. So when the invitation came, the realization that this blessing of restoration was moving me into a new phase in my life was both exciting and humbling.

I was anxious and nervous. I knew I was no longer the person I had been when I served and ministered in the public sphere prior to my fall. As I worked at picking up the pieces of my life, I slowly became accustomed to doing things that were no longer just about me. Instead, my thoughts for this first public event were focused on how I could use this opportunity to give God praise. I took time to thank God, praying in earnest as I sought His guidance and direction. I fasted for three days to make sure that 'self' did not pollute what God wanted accomplished. I felt refreshed and as each day passed, I felt more emboldened and confident that I had received this invitation for a reason and a purpose. Many past sermons came to mind, quickly taking form and then being shaped for this upcoming conference. Yet for some reason I was unsettled. As I would put a few final touches to the message, I would shake my head and toss away what I had written –it just wasn't the right sermon. I wrote and rewrote more sermons in those few days then I had in the past several months, yet I knew in my heart that not one of them was what God wanted me to preach. I needed to step into a new area of ministry, but I did not know if I had the faith and strength to

> " ...but I did not know if I had the faith and strength to do so.

do so. For God had spoken to me in prayer, saying, "Go and share... go and share your past!" I trembled at the thought. I did not want to be so transparent and vulnerable. I truly appreciated and was thankful for God's forgiveness. I was grateful He had met every need as I journeyed back to a place of restoration – but I wasn't ready to go 'live'. I was not yet ready to accept His call and His purpose for my life in this manner.

Every time I spoke about my failure, it presented me with my painful past. The emotions attached to this difficult time seemed unbearable at times, so why dredge it all back up? Because God wanted me to share my failure with others. Concerning this point, I had been doing some volunteer work, meeting with small churches to help them to put their organization into a more streamlined order. I would reaffirm what they were doing right while exposing those areas in which there was room for improvement. I would share only those parts of my story which emphasized the need for doing things in order. I would speak to pastors and church leadership, helping them to see the necessity of implementing bylaws and pointing out the need to operate according to these laws. I would explain why all money should be accounted for and handled not only in a legal manner, but within ethical boundaries.

For many of the churches I assisted, these issues were a given , but as I continued to share, more churches began to reveal problematic issues

> For many of the churches I assisted, these issues were a given...

that were blatantly evident to me. I was concerned about their exposure to potential lawsuits and even possible criminal convictions. Thankfully, every pastor and leader who heard my testimony and listened to the issues I exposed, made the necessary changes. I could see how my ministry was being shaped to help those who, either out of ignorance or arrogance – or a combination of both – needed to hear my testimony.

I was reminded of some research work I had done concerning a Prison Fellowship organization, with which I had considered seeking employment. The founder, Chuck Colson, was an aide to President Richard Nixon. Because of his role and responsibilities, he was caught up in the infamous Watergate scandal that was covered in every major news network. When the investigation was complete, Mr. Colson was found guilty and imprisoned. Colson said:

*"I thought my opportunity to accomplish anything really significant in my life was over once I was in prison and public enemy number one."* However, *"in the past 27 years since I've been out of prison, **I've seen how God has used my broken experience for His greatest glory.** ... Anything said about me has to be a reflection of the great things God has done, not Chuck Colson. I'm able to do what I do today because of the greatest failure of my life."*[320]

(emphasis added)

Jesus told a man who had just been healed from demon possession, *"Return to thine own house, and shew how great things God hath done unto thee."*[321] The verses preceding this story explain how this man lived as an outcast, tormented, and naked for many years in the tombs of Gadara. And on this particular day as Jesus stepped out of a boat, this man saw Jesus and rushed toward him and fell on his knees and begged for God's mercy on his life. Even from within the depravity of his possession, God allowed him a moment of sanity. This man could see the hope that stood

> " This man could see the hope that stood before him in Jesus.

before him in Jesus, and he cried out for Christ's mercy , knowing he would be released from his years of torment. Jesus heard his plea and in turn, He commanded the demons to leave the man. The legion of demons begged Jesus for permission to enter into a herd of swine. When His permission was granted, they ran off a cliff and drowned in the lake.

This demon-possessed man was healed both physically and spiritually. This man was filled with gratitude for what the Lord had just done. He begged Jesus for the opportunity to go with Him and stay at his side, but Jesus had another purpose for this man's life. Instead, Jesus told this man to go and share his story with others, and that is precisely what he did. All the years that this man had been possessed, and the terrible burden of his torment, would now become a powerful story of God's transformation. Family members, who were once ashamed, now marveled at the goodness of God. Those who spoke about the crazy naked man in the tombs now stood in awe as they listened intently to a man in his right mind talk about the love and mercy of a living God. It was the dreadful ordeal of this man's past, in combination with the healing which took place in his life that became the foundation of God's purpose for his life. A life he could never have imagined. **He was living proof of the miraculous life-changing power of Jesus Christ .**

Because this man was willing to share his story with others, it became a testimony that had more power for transforming the lives of others than a sweet Sunday morning sermon. Consider the countless number of people who turned to Christ as a result of this man, formerly naked and demon-possessed. All because he fearlessly went out to tell others about his terrible past, a past which encapsulated within it the seeds of his redemption. This man was used to reveal to others the great purpose God had, not only for his own life, but for those who also found themselves in a broken place.

I have often told others that people can debate and dispute Scripture with me all day long. They can deny prophecy and even deny the divinity of Christ, but no person can factually deny or ignore the transformative power of God in my life. Most often, it is the pain, adversity, and

>  Most often, it is the pain, adversity, and brokeness of our lives that God uses...

brokenness of our lives that God uses as a platform , allowing others to see the restorative power and faithfulness exhibited through who we have become in Christ. The truth that God really does take what the devil meant for evil, turning it to His own use for good, is what the world can see in your story. Your personal testimony, which details where you have been, where you are at presently, and where you are going, may well be the key ingredient that leads to redemption in the life of someone else.

In sharing my story, I've learned that whether or not I wanted to share my story did not matter. What mattered is the simple fact that it has always been God's desire and purpose for me to do so. **God will never waste any experience,** good or bad . He does not waste any pain from our past, choosing rather to use our pain as a healing ointment for others who are currently broken and in a painful place.

As I stood that evening before more than one thousand ministers, their families, and church members, I was about to deliver a message from God – but it would not be like any I had ever delivered before. I was a nervous wreck. Part of me felt like this was the beginning of the end. What would people think? Especially those who did not know about me?

How would this message be received? Would I have to relive the pain of the past? At the very moment in which I was being introduced, the Lord led my mind to 2 Corinthians 12, where the Apostle Paul had presented a complaint to God about a thorn in his flesh:

*"And lest I should be exalted above measure through the abundance of the revelations, there was given to me a thorn in the flesh, the messenger of Satan to buffet me, lest I should be exalted above measure. For this thing I besought the Lord thrice, that it might depart from me. And he said unto me, My grace is sufficient for thee: for my strength is made perfect in weakness."* – 2 Corinthians 12:7-8 and a partial rendering of verse 9 (KJV)

Paul brings his complaint to God three times. This is an interesting point, but what the Lord showed me regarding this thorn in Paul's flesh, and the reason why God chose not to remove it, is simply lest Paul, *"should be exalted above measure."* God allowed the thorn in Paul's flesh

> God allowed the thorn in Paul's flesh to remain there to keep Paul humble.

to remain there to keep Paul humble. When one considers the life of the Apostle Paul, one of two things always happened no matter where he went. He created either a riot or a revival! He always stirred things up, and as a result, God used Paul to write two-thirds of the New Testament. He was a very well educated man with a very strong nature, who could perhaps have started believing that he was something special within his own humanity. Paul also reveals in his words that this thorn in the flesh was from the messenger of Satan. In this we begin to realize that just like Job, God allowed Paul to be afflicted by Satan's messenger for His own divine purpose, not the purpose of the enemy.

None of us like to live in pain. We could easily list all the reasons why we would be better off without a specific affliction. Paul sought the Lord three times and God would not remove it. It stands to reason that God's purpose for the Apostle Paul included the building of his character, and in doing so, pushed away the spirit of pride that was trying to squirm into his life. Instead of having that affliction removed, God supplied

> Instead of having that affliction removed, God supplied greater grace and strength.

greater grace and strength. Paul in turned learned that God's strength is made perfect in our weakness.

From that night of sharing my testimony in a large public forum to this current moment, I cannot say it has been easy. I know that I am not required to wear my past failure on my sleeve for all to see, nor do I have to introduce myself by that failure, but I have learned that I must go and share it as the Lord directs. **I can testify that after each time of sharing, a refreshing element has been injected into my spiritual life , and it has been a tremendous blessing and reminder to me of how great my God is.** As I reflect on where I have come from, where I am now, and the possibilities that lie before me, it gives me greater strength to go and share the beauty of my restoration. God truly has transformed my life. He took the broken person I used to be, and began to mold me into something better than I was so I could serve His divine purpose. He continues to mold and shape me into a vessel that will hopefully always be worthy of His purpose.

God has a plan and great purpose for you! He has already prepared a beautiful future for you, which will gradually unfold as you learn to trust and believe in Him. **It is not in spite of our past that God reaches out to us... it is because of our past that He stands at the door and knocks .** As you open that door and invite him in, you will find that your latter days will be greater than your former days.[322]

206 Broken

# Conclusion
## In All Things God Works For The Good Of Those Who Love Him[319]

*"And we know that all things work together for good to them that love God, to them who are the called according to his purpose."*
– **Romans 8:28**

In the midst of my own brokenness, God assured me that *"all things work together for good to them that love God."* What a journey – from the public revelation of my failure to a place of complete brokenness; from a place of utter despair and feelings of rejection to that place of gratitude and inner peace in Christ. It truly has been a journey that at times felt too long and arduous, yet so necessary in God's plan for my restoration. My journey is not over, yet today my life

> " My journey is not over, yet today my life is a reflection of the power of God's restoration.

is a reflection of the power of God's restoration. I have learned through Christ to pick up the pieces, give them all to Him, and let the Lord mold me into His vessel.

As you stand in that broken state, you can be assured – not only by my personal testimony, but through powerful guiding Scriptures; illustrations of individuals in the Bible who failed God, yet were restored; and practical action steps – that God's promises are just as real and true for you! In this concluding chapter, I would like to summarize a few of the life lessons I have learned from my personal failures. These have all been referenced in different chapters, but in this final chapter, I would like to establish that all the information you have read is interwoven, and that the restoration process you have embarked upon has been designed by God through Scripture for you and your journey.

I will also share a few Scriptural records that will help you to grasp the magnitude of God's love for us, and the joy it brings Him when we turn to Him for restoration after experiencing failure. The most important revelation I received during my personal transformation is the knowledge that no matter how great our failure – even spectacular failings that result from wickedness and sin – that these failings can and will be used by God, who will reshape the final result for the good of those who love Him.

This magnificent truth is perhaps best illustrated by the story of Adam and Eve (related in chapter fifteen), who committed humanity's first sin by choosing to disobey God. God knew in advance that they would sin, and yet He allowed them the freedom to make that choice. If God had not allowed them to choose their own path, humanity would have been like innocent children until God imparted to them the crucial knowledge of good and evil. I honestly believe that in God's own timing, we would have been gently introduced to this knowledge, but He gave us free will, which allowed us the option to decide for ourselves how we would acquire this knowledge. I call this knowledge crucial because without it, we would never have attained the wisdom that allows us to knowingly choose God above the deception continually thrust at us by Satan. Without first acquiring the knowledge of good and evil, how would we ever have been able to distinguish between the choices that sustain life on this planet (and beyond) and those which destroy it?

**The sin of disobedience threw the world into turmoil, alienating humanity from walking with God in the fullness of His glory as we were created.** He allowed Adam and Eve to choose their own path, but in His love for them, He had already prepared a plan of redemption.[324]

This plan, filled with grace they did not deserve, released Adam and Eve from the mental and spiritual anguish they must have initially felt... imagine knowing that your sin would cause such dire hardship to your children and your children's children down through the ages! They were released from being utterly crushed by their failure because they heard God's promise that the seed of Eve's womb would bring a Savior who would redeem humanity from the curse sin had placed upon them.[325] Not only would the Savior restore human beings to the former glory Adam and Eve had experienced in Eden, but they would inherit a covenant superior to the one they had broken with God.[326] Humanity would receive a high priest superior in every way,[327] having experienced the same temptations Adam and Eve had faced, but without succumbing to these temptations. While human beings are still born into sin by nature of their genetic inheritance, after the death and resurrection of Jesus Christ we now have a choice to accept the joint inheritance of Christ,[328] offered to us by His Father.

Think for a moment about why the father of the Prodigal son was so overjoyed at seeing his wayward son return home after traveling in foreign lands. This man had two sons, and upon the request of his younger son, had given him an early inheritance.[329] This son, after receiving the portion of goods that fell to him, *"took his journey into a far country, and there wasted his substance with riotous living."*[330] The young man was finally reduced to tending a herd of swine.[331] At this point he recognized his failure, which had been brought about by an immoral lifestyle. Scripture then tells us that, *"when he came to himself,"*[332] he decided to return to his father, hoping to be hired as a servant.[333] There were specific laws governing the division of inheritances in Jewish

> There were specific laws governing the division of inheritances in Jewish society...

society during the days Jesus walked the earth. The oldest brother would receive a double share[334] of the father's inheritance, while the other brothers would receive a single share. In this case, because there were two brothers, the older brother would receive two thirds of the estate, while the younger brother would receive one third.[335] The thing about an inheritance is that children usually wait for their parents to die before demanding what, in this case, would be one third of the father's estate. Irrespective of the father's possible need for the portion of goods his son was asking for while he yet lived, this rascal claimed his portion and then squandered it.

I can't help noticing a few similarities between the story of the prodigal son and that of Adam. I contend that in the fullness of God's timing, Adam would have received the knowledge of good and evil. Yet

> Both men fail miserably by refusing to honor the law.

he took that which had been forbidden to him to appease his own self-gratification. Both men take something from their respective fathers before the gift is properly bestowed upon them. Both men act on selfish motives, and both lose their inheritance. Adam is sent out of Eden and the prodigal is reduced to a state of despair in which he craves "the husks"[336] that the swine ate, but is not even able to partake of this to alleviate his hunger. Both men fail miserably by refusing to honor the law – Adam refused to honor the one rule given to him by God when he chose to eat the forbidden fruit; the prodigal refused to honor the balance of his father's life (and the natural law of death), taking that which did not yet belong to him. In both cases, the fathers do not prevent their sons from exercising their will. In both cases the selfish desires of the sons lead to their undoing.

What is interesting to note, and very relevant to every person who has been broken by sin, is the response of God to Adam's fear and nakedness, and the response of the prodigal son's father to his son's shame and poor attire. After informing the serpent and the two humans of the consequences of their sin, **Scripture reveals that,** "*Unto Adam also and to his wife did the Lord God make coats of skins, and clothed them.*"[337] Where did these skins come from? It is naturally assumed that God sacrificed some animals so he could cover the shame and nakedness of His beloved children. Many Bible scholars consider this gift of clothing a foreshadowing of Christ's sacrifice on the cross,[338] which enables us to once more wear His robe of righteousness.[339] In the case of the prodigal son, "*he was yet a great way off,*" when "*his father saw him, and had compassion, and ran, and fell on his neck, and kissed him.*"[340] The son had decided in advance that he would tell his father he had sinned, and that because he no longer felt worthy to be called his son, he would entreat his father to hire him as a servant.[341] But before he was able to ask his father to hire him as a servant, the father said to his servants:

"*Bring forth the best robe, and put it on him; and put a ring on his hand, and shoes on his feet: 23 And bring hither the fatted calf, and kill it; and let us eat, and be merry: 24 For this my son was dead, and is alive again; he was lost, and is found. And they began to be merry.*"[342]

Remember that Jesus told this story to illustrate His Father's joy at receiving one lost sinner who has repented.[343] He actually told three

> ...Jesus told this story to illustrate His Father's joy at receiving one lost sinner...

consecutive stories with the same basic theme running through them: the parable of the lost sheep;[344] the parable of the lost coin;[345] and the parable of the lost (prodigal) son.[346] The theme that links all three parables is an explicit illustration of God's love for us and His willingness to forgive us no matter what we have done.[347] Just prior to Jesus relating these parables, *"the tax collectors and sinners were all gathering around to hear Jesus."*[348] Noticing this, "the Pharisees and the teachers of the law muttered, 'This man welcomes sinners and eats with them.'"[349] It is to this group of religious men that Jesus directs the parables. He starts out by saying: *"Suppose one of you..."*[350] He then goes on to tell them the three parables. All three parables revolve around the subject of recovering the

> All three parables revolve around the subject of recovering the lost...

lost, which is the implicit explanation of why Jesus receives sinners and eats with them: they are lost, and He wants to recover them.[351]

Recognizing the truth and beauty of this information will help you to accept the fact that no sin is too great for God to forgive, and there is no failure so great that God will refuse you restoration. In fact, God recognizes immediately when you do finally come to your senses, and like the prodigal's father, eagerly awaits your return while you are *"yet a great way off."*[352] He has *"compassion,"*[353] on you, and He runs to embrace you, kiss you, and welcome you home.

Another aspect of this parable relates to how those of us who are meant to be clothed in the righteousness of Christ – especially those in positions of leadership – should respond to our brothers and sisters who seek restoration. The older brother, who had faithfully served his father through the years, and had not at any time *"transgressed"* his *"commandment,"*[354] was *"angry"*[355] at his father's lavish treatment of his younger brother. He complained that his father had never so much as offered him a goat "kid," that he "might make merry"[356] with his friends. What the older brother did not take into account is the fact that he had always been with his father, and therefore, everything his father owned actually belonged to him.³⁵⁷ He was already experiencing the joy of his ultimate inheritance. His father had to point out to him the essence of his own (fatherly) joy, and the reason for his celebration : "*It was meet that*

> " His father had to point out to him the essence of his own (fatherly) joy...

*we should make merry, and be glad: for this thy brother was dead, and is alive again; and was lost, and is found.*"³⁵⁸

In a way, the reaction of this older brother brings to mind the ordeal I suffered at the hands of leadership when I first sought restoration. Rather than embracing me, and encouraging me to put on a fresh robe of righteousness, all they could see was how my sin would affect their lives, what they thought was theirs and the impact on their ministries. The anger of the older brother in this parable essentially reduces his character, causing it to reflect the same selfishness to which his younger brother had originally fallen prey.

Have you perhaps noticed a recurring pattern among those who have experienced failure due to sin? **Just about every Bible character we have referenced in this book has failed because they have fallen prey to selfishness.** Samson insisted on marrying a Philistine, and after inadvertently bringing about her death,³⁵⁹ he began courting a Philistine woman named Delilah, who harassed him endlessly to tell her the secret of his strength. Being a Nazarite from birth, Samson knew he shouldn't have been sleeping with the enemy, but he was used to doing as he pleased. He was self-centered and selfish. His selfishness eventually led to his death. Scripture even tells us that "*she pressed him daily with her words, and urged him, so that his soul was vexed unto death;...*"³⁶⁰ To find relief from Delilah's nagging, Samson gave up the secret of his strength. He allowed himself to be bullied into selfishly seeking relief from her badgering, rather than honoring God by keeping the source of his strength secret.

King David also experienced a phase of self-centered introspection which, going by today's jargon, would probably be called a midlife crisis.[361] I'm sure God would have overlooked him neglecting his duty to lead Israel into war, especially if he had been meditating on the Word of the Lord, but instead, David found himself meditating on Bathsheba, the wife of another man. This phase of self-centered introspection soon turned into a selfish demand to have Bathsheba presented to him! Every step the king took from this point on, up to the death of the child that

> Every step the king took...broadened the pathway of his sin.

was born from his adultery, broadened the pathway of his sin. The more deeply he engraved the neural pathways in his brain – through reinforcing and strengthening these sinful patterns by repetition[362] – the more difficult it became to extract himself from sin. Thus, the pattern of sin became more intricately intertwined into David's spirit through his own selfish choices.

The Apostle Peter's denial of Christ on the night of his illegal trial was also selfishly motivated. Fearing for his life, Peter denied knowing the same Man of whom he had previously said: *"Thou art the Christ, the Son of the living God."*[363] In His capacity as a human being, the fear of a brutal death had also surfaced in the thoughts of Jesus, yet the way in which He dealt with this fear reveals the selfless will of Christ as opposed to the selfish wills of Peter, Samson and David.

Jesus prayed: *"Father, if thou be willing, remove this cup from me: nevertheless not my will, but thine, be done."*[364] Herein lies a critical lesson for every person on earth: if you are not striving to enact the Father's will in every aspect of your life, you are more than likely living selfishly in those areas you have not given over to His will. **Remember that what we do in secret are seeds planted in our souls.** If these seeds are being watered by the *"fountain of living waters,"*[365] you can rest assured you are in the Father's will. If you water them in secret, knowing they do not conform to the pattern of righteousness, they will grow among thorns and thistles that choke the Word of God[366] in your life.

There is a moment of conscious decision to every sin... in the moment King David became aware of Bathsheba on a rooftop below him he had to make a choice. Would he, the commander of Israel's army, already in dereliction of this duty, turn his eyes from the spectacle before him? Or would he indulge in voyeurism?

Concerning his integrity, David had had an almost impeccable track record to this point. The only inconsistency Scripture reveals is David's decision not to attend the war he had sent Israel's army to fight. From this weakened moral position, David took the next step into actual sin, turning his life into a skein of lies and deception. Each sin was compounded by the next, culminating in heartache, death, and the loss of peace in David's life. What David had done in private (adultery)

> Each sin was compounded by the next, culminating in heartache, death...

was brought upon him publicly when his son Absalom raped all ten of David's concubines.[367] From the moment David chose his destiny with Bathsheba, his story reads as a litany of human failure, one event setting off the next. Yet Scripture reveals that God worked this tangled mess of sin to His own glory.

God recognizes our humanity. He works with us in our weaknesses. David's saving grace was his recognition of one simple revelation: what you have done does not have to be who you become. **David grasped the truth that God uses failure to hone people into sharper tools for His service.** This knowledge encouraged King David to run toward God rather than away from Him during crisis. He offered no excuses for his sin. He simply admitted that he had sinned against God.[368] By identifying his sin, David took the first step in picking up the pieces of his brokenness. The second step he took was to worship God in the midst of his failure.[369] In the midst of your own failure, remember the Biblical requirement to forgive others just as you expect God to forgive you. If ever you begin to doubt that you are loved and forgiven, refer back to the exercise you completed in chapter seven, which helped you to differentiate between all the projected truths and untruths about yourself and your failure.

Hold onto the belief that you can be trusted again, and that you should be given another chance! All you have to do is work responsibly toward meeting the conditions and requirements that will put you in a position to receive this blessing. Remember that your credibility can be rebuilt, but it requires a developed plan of action, honesty, vulnerability, and time. As Christ becomes the foundation of your life, you will begin to appreciate the freedom that accountability will bring.

> Remember that your credibility can be rebuilt, but it requires a developed plan...

Being accountable means that people will no longer be unsure of your integrity. When you hold yourself to account, you become an open book for other people to study. In this, you have the opportunity to shine the light of Christ into the world, freeing others from the bondage of darkness. Rebuilding your credibility will take time, but this exercise is certainly attainable with the help of your heavenly Father.

Once you have identified the unusable pieces of your life, such as your besmirched character and integrity, you can start rebuilding these crucial aspects of righteous living. **Pay special attention to healing any rifts that may have developed as a result of your failure , especially with close family members and other loved ones.** Pieces of your life that represent the social and business positions you hold, as well as your status in the community, can be worked back into a place where your dignity is restored. It just takes time, effort, and trust in God. Remember to be delicate in your dealings with people affected by your failure, especially those who you consider friends or even only acquaintances. Be careful lest they use your failure for their own gain or for retribution. Be careful in dealing with the affected people, but do not operate from a base of fear, for you have already asked God's forgiveness. Once you have turned your life, your failure, and all your broken pieces over to the Master Potter, He will remove the marred areas and recreate you into a superior vessel.

If you are involved in leadership activities, it is important that you recognize the critical role you play in working with those who have failed. Spiritually mature Christians are required to guide and assist the fallen in their restoration process , while scrupulously maintaining their own integrity and humility. You are there to represent the redemptive work of Christ in the life of the broken. With human leaders serving as

> Spiritually mature Christians are required to guide and assist the fallen...

an example, they in turn can be restored to a state where they magnify and replicate the mercy of God through their own constructive service to others. Be sure you have all the necessary Scriptures available to guide those who look to you to help them through this process. This will ensure that all the issues that have an adverse effect on the broken are properly and Biblically addressed. Be sure to include those affected by their failure when helping them look into areas of forgiveness and restitution. It will most likely be helpful to explain that no two circumstances are alike, and that the steps to restoration are not a cookie-cutter process. Rather, you as the spiritual leader must discern the specifics of what is needed.

This will help you to work in more detail with the broken, using a strategy that is tailored exclusively to him or her.

For those of you who are experiencing failure, take time to consider the possible reasons for you needing to grow and learn through this hardship. Take comfort in the knowledge that perhaps, like with Joseph, God is not yet willing to give an inexperienced individual a significant anointing without some major internal changes. Embrace this personal transformation you are currently processing. **God is able to use the trauma of your circumstances to turn your latent potential into something actual and real for the benefit of His kingdom.** The key to your personal transformation is co-operation with the Holy Spirit. Trust God and take Him at His word, but do not stress about results you cannot measure. God does not measure time, but human growth.

> The key to your personal transformation is co-operation with the Holy Spirit.

Reconsidering the story of Adam and Eve, we begin to understand God's detailed plan for humanity's redemption. In our understanding of this plan we are given a glimpse of how God is able to turn a cosmic disaster into a successful process that leads to eternal life. Knowing this, it becomes much simpler to trust that God will turn our private and public disasters into successful processes of restoration that lead to wisdom and greater faith in God. **Sin provides the occasion for God's grace, bringing repentance and reconciliation.** These aspects in turn lead to a more intimate union with God.

I sincerely hope this has been a journey of self-discovery that has laid a foundation of hope in your spirit. I pray you will implement the steps necessary for change to take place in your life. Do your best to align yourself with a spiritually mature leader or ministry team to help you grow in your walk or renewed walk with Christ.

> Failure is not final!

Failure is not final! **Failure, and the state of being broken, is only a temporary setback.** With the guidance of Jesus Christ, you who have been broken by failure are definitely able to pick up the pieces of your lives after the fall.

I began by praying for you and now I wish to conclude in a prayer of thanksgiving for you:

> *Lord, as I close with these final words, I pray You will allow the transparency of my failure and subsequent restoration, along with the many examples and promises of your Word that expounded upon in the pages of this book, become the spark that ignites hope into the life of the reader. Thank you for guiding them and leading them along the path of their personal journey of transformation. I pray they will receive the revelation of the depth and breadth of Your love for them. I plead Your precious blood over their life as You begin anew in them. In Jesus name I pray, Amen.*

220 Broken

# Endnotes

1    Isaiah 42:3 The Holy Bible, English Standard Version (ESV) Copyright © 2001 by Crossway Bibles, a publishing ministry of Good News Publishers.
2    Galatians 6:1 King James Version (KJV) by Public Domain
3    Romans 3:23 King James Version (KJV) by Public Domain
4    Chapter One
5    Romans 3:23 King James Version (KJV) by Public Domain
6    Paraphrase of Psalm 51:5 King James Version (KJV) by Public Domain
7    Proverbs 24:16 King James Version (KJV) by Public Domain
8    Abraham Lincoln's Road To The White House http://pastorappreciationblog.com/2012/08/11/abraham-lincolns-road-to-the-white-house/
9    Chapter Two
10    Opie & Opie (1997), pp. 213–5.
11    Partial rendering of 1 Timothy 6:15-16 King James Version (KJV) by Public Domain
12    Galatians 5:9 King James Version (KJV) by Public Domain
13    Chapter Three
14    "What is repentance and is it necessary for salvation?" http://www.gotquestions.org/repentance.html
15    Luke 3:8-14; Acts 3:19 King James Version (KJV) by Public Domain
16    "What is repentance and is it necessary for salvation?" http://www.gotquestions.org/repentance.html
17    Matthew 3:8 King James Version (KJV) by Public Domain
18    Paraphrase of Job 2:9 King James Version (KJV) by Public Domain
19    Chapter Four
20    1 Samuel 13:14 King James Version (KJV) by Public Domain
21    2 Samuel 11 King James Version (KJV) by Public Domain
22    Partial rendering of 2 Samuel 12:13 King James Version (KJV) by Public Domain
23    Denis Waitley. BrainyQuote.com, Xplore Inc, 2014. http://www.brainyquote.com/quotes/quotes/d/deniswaitl125740.html, accessed December 5, 2014.
24    Matthew 14:25 King James Version (KJV) by Public Domain
25    Matthew 14:30 King James Version (KJV) by Public Domain
26    Matthew 16:22 King James Version (KJV) by Public Domain

27    Matthew 16:16 King James Version (KJV) by Public Domain
28    Matthew 16:17 King James Version (KJV) by Public Domain
29    Matthew 16:23 King James Version (KJV) by Public Domain
30    Matthew 16:18 King James Version (KJV) by Public Domain
31    Matthew 17:1-5 King James Version (KJV) by Public Domain
32    Matthew 17:4 King James Version (KJV) by Public Domain
33    Matthew 17:5 King James Version (KJV) by Public Domain
34    Partial rendering of John 13:8 King James Version (KJV) by Public Domain
35    Matthew 26:40-43 King James Version (KJV) by Public Domain
36    Matthew 26:41 King James Version (KJV) by Public Domain
37    John 18:10 King James Version (KJV) by Public Domain
38    John 18:25-27 King James Version (KJV) by Public Domain
39    John 21:3 King James Version (KJV) by Public Domain
40    John 21:15-19 King James Version (KJV) by Public Domain
41    Galatians 2:11-14 King James Version (KJV) by Public Domain
42    Galatians 2:13 King James Version (KJV) by Public Domain
43    Acts 2:41 King James Version (KJV) by Public Domain
44    Judges 13:3 King James Version (KJV) by Public Domain
45    Nazirite |ˈnazəˌrīt| (also Nazarite) noun historical
an Israelite consecrated to the service of God, under vows to abstain from alcohol, let the hair grow, and avoid defilement by contact with corpses (Num. 6).
ORIGIN from Hebrew nāzīr 'consecrated one,' from nāzar 'to separate or consecrate oneself,' + -ite 1. Apple Dictionary Version 2.1.3 (80.4) Copyright © 2005–2009 Apple Inc. All rights reserved.
46    Judges 13:5 King James Version (KJV) by Public Domain
47    Nazarites, Arise!         http://ihop-atlanta.com/xwp/?p=48
48    Judges 16:22 King James Version (KJV) by Public Domain
49    Judges 13:5 King James Version (KJV) by Public Domain
50    Judges 16:28 King James Version (KJV) by Public Domain

51    1 Samuel 13:14 King James Version (KJV) by Public Domain
52    Chapter Five
53    http://www.brainyquote.com/quotes/quotes/t/theodorero163580.html
54    Romans 5:20 King James Version (KJV) by Public Domain
55    b (1) : a state of inability to perform a normal function <kidney failure>
— compare heart failure (2) : an abrupt cessation of normal functioning <a power failure> http://www.merriam-webster.com/dictionary/failure

# Endnotes

56    Wisdom to deal with failure, BMGC, 24th Nov 2013
http://www.slideshare.net/ylkhong/24th-nov-wisdom-to-deal-with-failure

57    For a more detailed consideration of these issues, see Lutzer's discussion of this on pages 20-26 of his excellent book,
Failure, The Backdoor to Success.
Failure: The Backdoor to Success Paperback – December, 1975 by Erwin W. Lutzer (Author), Howard G. Hendricks (Foreword)

58    1 Kings 11:4 King James Version (KJV) by Public Domain

59    1 Kings 11:12 King James Version (KJV) by Public Domain

60    1 Kings 11:13 King James Version (KJV) by Public Domain

61    1 Kings 11:5 King James Version (KJV) by Public Domain

62    1 Kings 11:7 King James Version (KJV) by Public Domain

63    Isaiah 51:6 King James Version (KJV) by Public Domain

64    Lamentations 3:22-23 King James Version (KJV) by Public Domain

65    Pastors on Moral Failures in Church Leadership: Don't Hide It By Lillian Kwon, Christian Post Reporter October 26, 2012|5:03 pm
http://www.christianpost.com/news/pastors-on-moral-failures-in-church-leadership-dont-hide-it-84013/

66    Ibid

67    Ibid

68    Ibid

69    Ibid

70    Luke 15:10 King James Version (KJV) by Public Domain
"Likewise, I say unto you, there is joy in the presence of the angels of God over one sinner that repenteth."

71    Pastors on Moral Failures in Church Leadership: Don't Hide It By Lillian Kwon, Christian Post Reporter October 26, 2012|5:03 pm
http://www.christianpost.com/news/pastors-on-moral-failures-in-church-leadership-dont-hide-it-84013/

72    Ibid

73    Chapter Six

74    Job 1:3 King James Version (KJV) by Public Domain

75    Job 1:20 King James Version (KJV) by Public Domain

76    How to Use Worship as a Way to Move Toward God during Life Challenges (http://www.prayerideas.org/wp/praying_for_needs/life-situations/how-to-use-worship-as-a- way-to-move-toward-god- during-life-challenges/) Copyright David E. Shelton All rights reserved.

77  Ibid
78  Hebrews 4:16 King James Version (KJV) by Public Domain
79  John 14:15 King James Version (KJV) by Public Domain
80  Paraphrase of Matthew 14:29 King James Version (KJV) by Public Domain
81  Paraphrase of Matthew 14:30 King James Version (KJV) by Public Domain
82  Partial rendering of Hebrews 13:5 King James Version (KJV) by Public Domain
83  The Grace of God in Our Lives, By Pastor William R. Cunningham August 7, 2005, For: Pursuing The Truth Ministries (http://www.pursuingthetruth.org/sermons/files/graceinlives.htm)
84  Ibid
85  Paraphrase of 2 Samuel 12:16-18 King James Version (KJV) by Public Domain
86  2 Samuel 12:13 King James Version (KJV) by Public Domain
87  Matthew 5:45 King James Version (KJV) by Public Domain
"That ye may be the children of your Father which is in heaven: for he maketh his sun to rise on the evil and on the good, and sendeth rain on the just and on the unjust."
88  Ephesians 2:8-9 King James Version (KJV) by Public Domain
89  Grace and Mercy (http://www.godsglory.org/devotional%20grace%20and%20mercy.htm)
90  According to the Vines Expository Dictionary of New Testament words – taken from: Grace and Mercy http://www.godsglory.org/devotional%20grace%20and%20mercy.htm
91  Grace and Mercy (http://www.godsglory.org/devotional%20grace%20and%20mercy.htm)
92  "Draw nigh to God, and he will draw nigh to you...." – James 4:8 King James Version (KJV) by Public Domain
93  Beliefnet – Inspirational Quotes – (Unknown quote) http://www.beliefnet.com/Quotes/Evangelical/U/Unknown/Grace-Is-When-God-Gives-Us-What-We-Dont-Deserve-A.aspx
94  Chapter Seven
95  Fifty Quotes on Forgiveness http://www.iloveulove.com/wisdom/50quotes.htm
96  2 Corinthians 5:17 King James Version (KJV) by Public Domain
97  Isaiah 66:2; Psalm 51:17 King James Version (KJV) by Public Domain
98  Partial rendering of Isaiah 57:15 King James Version (KJV) by Public Domain
99  "What does it mean to be contrite? What is contrition?" http://www.gotquestions.org/contrite-contrition.html

| | |
|---|---|
| 100 | Partial rendering of 2 Corinthians 12:9 King James Version (KJV) by Public Domain |
| 101 | Ibid |
| 102 | Mark 10:46-52 King James Version (KJV) by Public Domain |
| 103 | Mark 10:48 King James Version (KJV) by Public Domain |
| 104 | Mark 10:52 King James Version (KJV) by Public Domain |
| 105 | 1 John 1:9 King James Version (KJV) by Public Domain |
| 106 | Matthew 11:28 King James Version (KJV) by Public Domain |
| 107 | Matthew 24:35 King James Version (KJV) by Public Domain |
| 108 | 2 Corinthians 5:7 King James Version (KJV) by Public Domain |
| 109 | Romans 8:17 King James Version (KJV) by Public Domain |
| 110 | 1 John 4:4 King James Version (KJV) by Public Domain |
| 111 | 14 Quotes From Trash Talking Extraordinaire, Muhammad Ali http://www.rsvlts.com/2013/11/15/muhammad-ali-quotes/ |
| 112 | Ibid |
| 113 | John 1:9 King James Version (KJV) by Public Domain |
| 114 | Paraphrase of Romans 8:37 King James Version (KJV) by Public Domain |
| 115 | Chapter Eight |
| 116 | Partial rendering of Romans 8:28 King James Version (KJV) by Public Domain |
| 117 | Paraphrase of Genesis 37:28 King James Version (KJV) by Public Domain |
| 118 | Exodus 2:14 King James Version (KJV) by Public Domain |
| 119 | Genesis 29:31 King James Version (KJV) by Public Domain |
| 120 | Revelation 5:5 King James Version (KJV) by Public Domain |
| 121 | Genesis 29:35 King James Version (KJV) by Public Domain |
| 122 | Galatians 4:7; James 2:5; Titus 3:7 King James Version (KJV) by Public Domain |
| 123 | 2 Corinthians 5:21 King James Version (KJV) by Public Domain |
| 124 | John 14:27 King James Version (KJV) by Public Domain |
| 125 | Hebrews 13:5 King James Version (KJV) by Public Domain |
| 126 | A Man of The Word – The Life of G Campbell Morgan by Jill Morgan, Published 1951 by Fleming H Revell Co. |
| 127 | Ibid |
| 128 | Matthew 6:15 King James Version (KJV) by Public Domain |
| 129 | Paraphrase of Matthew 22:37-40 King James Version (KJV) by Public Domain |
| 130 | Matthew 18:23-35 King James Version (KJV) by Public Domain |
| 131 | Mark 11:25 King James Version (KJV) by Public Domain |
| 132 | Matthew 6:15 King James Version (KJV) by Public Domain |

133     Mark 11:24-25 King James Version (KJV) by Public Domain
134     John 15:5; 15:10; 15:12 King James Version (KJV) by Public Domain
135     1 John 3:14 King James Version (KJV) by Public Domain
136     John 14:21 King James Version (KJV) by Public Domain
137     John 15:10 King James Version (KJV) by Public Domain
138     Ephesians 4:23 King James Version (KJV) by Public Domain
139     Romans 12:2 King James Version (KJV) by Public Domain
140     Partial rendering of Proverbs 23:7 King James Version (KJV) by Public Domain
141     Amplified Bible (AMP) Copyright © 1954, 1958, 1962, 1964, 1965, 1987 by The Lockman Foundation
142 Jeremiah 29:11 King James Version (KJV) by Public Domain
143     Lloyd John Ogilvie http://www.lloydjohnogilvie.com/
144     2 ways to overcome the fear of rejection, February 10, 2013 http://kevinmartineau.ca/overcome-fear-of-rejection/
145     Proverbs 29:25 King James Version (KJV) by Public Domain
146 Matthew 28:19 King James Version (KJV) by Public Domain
147 The Lego Principle (pg 27) Joey Bonafacio Charisma House
148     Paraphrase of 2 Timothy 1:7 King James Version (KJV) by Public Domain
149     Partial rendering of Psalm 46:10 King James Version (KJV) by Public Domain
150 1 Kings 18 King James Version (KJV) by Public Domain
151 Paraphrase of 1 Kings 19: 11-12 King James Version (KJV) by Public Domain
152 Psalm 62:5-6 King James Version (KJV) by Public Domain
153     16. The Restoration of Elijah (1 Kings 19:5-18) https://bible.org/seriespage/16-restoration-elijah-1-kings-195-18
154     Chapter Nine
155     Brian Koslow Quotes http://thinkexist.com/quotation/the_more_you_are_willing_to_accept_responsibility/190423.html
156     2 Corinthians 5:17 King James Version (KJV) by Public Domain
157 http://www.un.org/millenniumgoals/bkgd.shtml
158     verb [ trans. ]
3 think about and begin to deal with (an issue or problem) : a fundamental problem has still to be addressed. Apple Dictionary Version 2.1.3 (80.4) Copyright © 2005–2009 Apple Inc. All rights reserved.
159     Paraphrase of Matthew 14:22-33 King James Version (KJV) by Public Domain
160 Chapter Ten

161	http://www.webster-dictionary.net/definition/broken
162	Apple Dictionary Version 2.1.3 (80.4) Copyright © 2005–2009 Apple Inc. All rights reserved.
163 2 Corinthians 4:7 King James Version (KJV) by Public Domain
164 Jeremiah 18:4 King James Version (KJV) by Public Domain
165 Deuteronomy 6:4 King James Version (KJV) by Public Domain
166 Partial rendering of 2 Corinthians 5:7 King James Version (KJV) by Public Domain
167 Paraphrase of Nehemiah 2:19 King James Version (KJV) by Public Domain
168	Chapter Eleven
169	1 John 4:4 King James Version (KJV) by Public Domain
170	Partial rendering of Proverbs 3:6 King James Version (KJV) by Public Domain
171	http://www.goodreads.com/quotes/6071-many-of-life-s-failures-are-people-who-did-not-realize
172	Chapter Twelve
173	3 Types of Change Your Brain Adapts: Reinforcing Behaviors, 1 of 3 By Athena Staik, Ph.D. http://blogs.psychcentral.com/relationships/2011/08/three-ways-your-brain-adapts-to-change-1-of-3/
174 Romans 6:23 King James Version (KJV) by Public Domain
175 2 Samuel 11:1 King James Version (KJV) by Public Domain
176 1 Samuel 21:4 King James Version (KJV) by Public Domain
177 Ibid
178 Paraphrase of 2 Samuel 12:16-17 King James Version (KJV) by Public Domain
179 Paraphrase of 1 Samuel 13:14 King James Version (KJV) by Public Domain
180	31. Failure Lapse, Not Collapse--A Biblical View of Failure (Luke 22:24-33; 54-62) https://bible.org/seriespage/31-failure-lapse-not-collapse-biblical-view-failure-luke-2224-33-54-62
181	Ibid
182	2 Samuel 12:20 King James Version (KJV) by Public Domain
183 2 Samuel 18:1-33 King James Version (KJV) by Public Domain
184	Paraphrase of Romans 8:28 King James Version (KJV) by Public Domain
185	C. S. Lewis, Mere Christianity pp. 167-168 C. S. Lewis Classics Edition published 2012 by Collins, a division of HarperCollinsPublishers
186	31. Failure Lapse, Not Collapse--A Biblical View of Failure (Luke 22:24-33; 54-62) https://bible.org/seriespage/31-failure-lapse-not-collapse-biblical-view-failure-luke-2224-33-54-62
187	Daniel 2:20-21 King James Version (KJV) by Public Domain

188   Paraphrase of 1 Peter 5:8 King James Version (KJV) by Public Domain
189   31. Failure Lapse, Not Collapse--A Biblical View of Failure (Luke 22:24-33; 54-62) https://bible.org/seriespage/31-failure-lapse-not-collapse-biblical-view-failure-luke-2224-33-54-62
190   31. Failure Lapse, Not Collapse--A Biblical View of Failure (Luke 22:24-33; 54-62) https://bible.org/seriespage/31-failure-lapse-not-collapse-biblical-view-failure-luke-2224-33-54-62
191   Ibid
192   2 Corinthians 12:7-10 King James Version (KJV) by Public Domain
193   Paraphrase of 2 Corinthians 12:9 King James Version (KJV) by Public Domain
194   31. Failure Lapse, Not Collapse--A Biblical View of Failure (Luke 22:24-33; 54-62) https://bible.org/seriespage/31-failure-lapse-not-collapse-biblical-view-failure-luke-2224-33-54-62
195   Paraphrase of Luke 22:34 King James Version (KJV) by Public Domain
196   Luke 22:33 King James Version (KJV) by Public Domain
197   31. Failure Lapse, Not Collapse--A Biblical View of Failure (Luke 22:24-33; 54-62) https://bible.org/seriespage/31-failure-lapse-not-collapse-biblical-view-failure-luke-2224-33-54-62
198   1 Peter 5:1-6 King James Version (KJV) by Public Domain
199   1 Peter 5:6 King James Version (KJV) by Public Domain
200   31. Failure Lapse, Not Collapse--A Biblical View of Failure (Luke 22:24-33; 54-62) https://bible.org/seriespage/31-failure-lapse-not-collapse-biblical-view-failure-luke-2224-33-54-62
201   Partial rendering of Luke 22:61 King James Version (KJV) by Public Domain
202   Partial rendering of Luke 22:62 King James Version (KJV) by Public Domain
203   John 21:15-17 King James Version (KJV) by Public Domain
204   Psalm 145:14 King James Version (KJV) by Public Domain
205   Chapter Thirteen
206   Matthew 3:8 King James Version (KJV) by Public Domain
207   Galatians 5:22-23 New International Version 2011 (NIV 2011)
208   Dec 27 - Twitter https://twitter.com/rwmartin63/status/549077224960184320
209   Acts 10:34 King James Version (KJV) by Public Domain
210   Jonah 3:10 King James Version (KJV) by Public Domain: "And God saw their works, that they turned from their evil way; and God repented of the evil, that he had said that he would do unto them; and he did it not."
211   Paraphrase of Romans 3:23 King James Version (KJV) by Public Domain 212

A Process For Biblical Restoration And Healing
http://www.ganttstreetbaptist.org/article.aspx?auid=6
213     Acts 15:36-40 King James Version (KJV) by Public Domain
214     Acts 15:39 King James Version (KJV) by Public Domain
215     Partial rendering of 2 Timothy 4:11 King James Version (KJV) by Public Domain
216     The five foundational steps I have outlined are based on the five steps that appear in an informative article called: A Process For Biblical Restoration And Healing.
The complete article can be sourced at: http://www.ganttstreetbaptist.org/article.aspx?auid=6
217     ttp://12step.org/the-12-steps/
218     Leviticus 6:5 King James Version (KJV) by Public Domain
219     Leviticus 6:1-6 King James Version (KJV) by Public Domain
220     Paraphrase of Galatians 6:1 King James Version (KJV) by Public Domain
221     Luke 15:11-32 King James Version (KJV) by Public Domain
222     Chapter Fourteen
223     Quotes On Transformation - Inspirational Quotes http://www.inspirationalquotes4u.com/ontransformation/index.html
224     Graham Cooke Verified account https://twitter.com/grahamcookebbh/status/425314103163617280
225     Psalm 105:16-22 King James Version (KJV) by Public Domain
226     Matthew Henry's Commentary on Psalm 105:16–22
227     Psalm 105:19 Amplified Bible (AMP) Copyright © 1954, 1958, 1962, 1964, 1965, 1987 by The Lockman Foundation
228     Matthew Henry's Commentary on Ps 105:16–22
229     Habakkuk 2:3 King James Version (KJV) by Public Domain
230     Psalm 105:19 NIV® Copyright © 1973, 1978, 1984, 2011 by Biblica, Inc.®
231 Graham Cooke Sermons - Visions http://hisloveworks.com/2014/02/08/brokeness-by-graham-cooke/
232     Ibid
233     Ibid
234     Ibid
235     Genesis 32:22-28 King James Version (KJV) by Public Domain
236     He [Jacob] was a con artist, a liar, and a manipulator. In fact, the name Jacob not only means "deceiver," but more literally it means "grabber." (http://www.gotquestions.org/Jacob-wrestling-with-God.html)

237	After Jacob's wrestle with the angel, when he demanded a blessing from the Lord, the angel pronounced a blessing upon him, and a new name to go with it: Isra-El, which can mean "He who prevails with God," or "May God prevail," depending on the context. http://christianity.stackexchange.com/questions/18587/why-did-god-change-jacobs-name-to-israel

238	Genesis 32:22-23 King James Version (KJV) by Public Domain

239	Graham Cooke Sermons - Visions http://hisloveworks.com/2014/02/08/brokeness-by-graham-cooke/

240	Genesis 42:21 King James Version (KJV) by Public Domain

241	Graham Cooke Sermons - Visions http://hisloveworks.com/2014/02/08/brokeness-by-graham-cooke/

242	Ibid

243	Ibid

244	Genesis 37:5-11 King James Version (KJV) by Public Domain

245	Genesis 37:11 King James Version (KJV) by Public Domain

246	Graham Cooke Sermons - Visions http://hisloveworks.com/2014/02/08/brokeness-by-graham-cooke/

247	Genesis 42:21 King James Version (KJV) by Public Domain

248	Graham Cooke Sermons - Visions http://hisloveworks.com/2014/02/08/brokeness-by-graham-cooke/

249	Ibid

250	Paraphrase of Genesis 42:24 King James Version (KJV) by Public Domain

251	Genesis 45:5-8 King James Version (KJV) by Public Domain

252	Paraphrase of Romans 8:28 King James Version (KJV) by Public Domain

253	John 12:27 King James Version (KJV) by Public Domain

254	John 12:28 King James Version (KJV) by Public Domain

255	Paraphrase of Isaiah 53:3 King James Version (KJV) by Public Domain

256	1 Thessalonians 5:18 King James Version (KJV) by Public Domain

257	Graham Cooke Sermons - Visions http://hisloveworks.com/2014/02/08/brokeness-by-graham-cooke/

258	Ibid

259	1 Samuel 24:1-7; and 1 Samuel 26:7-12 King James Version (KJV) by Public Domain

260	Graham Cooke Sermons - Visions http://hisloveworks.com/2014/02/08/brokeness-by-graham-cooke/

261	Ibid

262   Paraphrase of 1 Corinthians 10:13 King James Version (KJV) by Public Domain
263   Matthew Henry's Commentary on 1 Corinthians 10:6-14
264   Paraphrase of Jeremiah 29:11 King James Version (KJV) by Public Domain
265   Graham Cooke Sermons - Visions
http://hisloveworks.com/2014/02/08/brokeness-by-graham-cooke/
266 Chapter Fifteen
267   Mahatma Gandhi writes in My Non-Violence, a collection of his work produced by Navajivan, the publishing house he founded in 1929.
Fail Better: Lessons from Gandhi Before India - Biographile http://www.biographile.com/fail-better-lessons-from-gandhi-before-india/30990/
268   Proverbs 2:6 King James Version (KJV) by Public Domain
269   Proverbs 2:6; Daniel 2:20; Ephesians 1:17; Proverbs 9:10 King James Version (KJV) by Public Domain
270   "Is the king of Tyre prophecy in Ezekiel 28 referring to Satan?" http://www.gotquestions.org/King-of-Tyre.html
271   Ibid
272    Partial rendering of Revelation 22:13 King James Version (KJV) by Public Domain 273 Luke 10:18 King James Version (KJV) by Public Domain
274   Revelation 12:7-9 King James Version (KJV) by Public Domain 275 Ephesians 6:12 King James Version (KJV) by Public Domain
"For we wrestle not against flesh and blood, but against principalities, against powers, against the rulers of the darkness of this world, against spiritual wickedness in high places."
276   Paraphrase of Genesis 3:3 King James Version (KJV) by Public Domain
277   Bob Deffinbaugh
https://bible.org/users/bob-deffinbaugh
278   5. The Fall of Man in God's Perfect Plan
https://bible.org/seriespage/5-fall-man-gods-perfect-plan
279   Revelation 21:2 King James Version (KJV) by Public Domain
280   5. The Fall of Man in God's Perfect Plan
https://bible.org/seriespage/5-fall-man-gods-perfect-plan
281   The Serpent of Paradise: The Incredible Story of How Satan's Rebellion Serves God's Purposes - eBook
By: Erwin W. Lutzer Moody Publishers / 1986 / ePub (http://www.christianbook.com/serpent-paradise-incredible- rebellion-serves-purposes/erwin-lutzer/9781575677309/pd/16650EB?)

282  Matthew 8:31 King James Version (KJV) by Public Domain
283  The Serpent of Paradise: The Incredible Story of How Satan's Rebellion Serves God's Purposes - eBook
By: Erwin W. Lutzer Moody Publishers / 1986 / ePub (http://www.christianbook.com/serpent-paradise-incredible- rebellion-serves-purposes/erwin-lutzer/9781575677309/pd/16650EB?)
284  Paraphrase of Genesis 3:10 King James Version (KJV) by Public Domain
285  Proverbs 9:10 King James Version (KJV) by Public Domain
286  Genesis 3:7 King James Version (KJV) by Public Domain 287 Psalm 8:5 King James Version (KJV) by Public Domain
288  Psalm 8:5 Amplified Bible (AMP) Copyright © 1954, 1958, 1962, 1964, 1965, 1987 by The Lockman Foundation
289  1 Corinthians 6:3 King James Version (KJV) by Public Domain
290  Why were Adam and Eve "afraid" of being naked after they sinned? http://www.answers2prayer.org/bible_questions/Answers/sin/afraid.html   Ibid
291  Paraphrase of Galatians 3:26-27 King James Version (KJV) by Public Domain
292  Galatians 3:27 New International Version 2011 (NIV 2011)
293  Referenced in Isaiah 61:10 King James Version (KJV) by Public Domain
294  5. The Fall of Man in God's Perfect Plan
https://bible.org/seriespage/5-fall-man-gods-perfect-plan
295  Ibid
296  Isaiah 53:3-6 King James Version (KJV) by Public Domain
297  5. The Fall of Man in God's Perfect Plan
https://bible.org/seriespage/5-fall-man-gods-perfect-plan
298  Genesis 3:16 King James Version (KJV) by Public Domain
299  Paraphrase of Genesis 3:15 King James Version (KJV) by Public Domain 300  5. The Fall of Man in God's Perfect Plan
https://bible.org/seriespage/5-fall-man-gods-perfect-plan
301  Paraphrase of Genesis 3:17-18 King James Version (KJV) by Public Domain
302  Paraphrase of Genesis 3:19 King James Version (KJV) by Public Domain
303  5. The Fall of Man in God's Perfect Plan
https://bible.org/seriespage/5-fall-man-gods-perfect-plan
304  5. The Fall of Man in God's Perfect Plan
https://bible.org/seriespage/5-fall-man-gods-perfect-plan
305 Romans 11:32 King James Version (KJV) by Public Domain
306 5. The Fall of Man in God's Perfect Plan
https://bible.org/seriespage/5-fall-man-gods-perfect-plan

307 Ibid
308     Failure Is Feedback: How 5 Billionaires had To Fail To Succeed
309     Ibid
310     Ibid
311     Ibid
By Victor Balasa. Filed in People, Web 2.0 (http://www.hongkiat.com/blog/fail-to-succeed-billionaires/)
312     John 9:7 King James Version (KJV) by Public Domain 313 John 9:2 King James Version (KJV) by Public Domain 314 John 9:3 King James Version (KJV) by Public Domain 315 John 9:38 King James Version (KJV) by Public Domain 316 John 9:34 King James Version (KJV) by Public Domain
317 If God Is Good by Randy Alcorn Copyright © 2009 by Randy Alcorn.
318 How God Uses Suffering for His Glory
Five reasons we must face affliction. By Randy Alcorn http://www.familylife.com/articles/topics/marriage/challenges/hardship-and-suffering/how-god-uses-suffering-for-his- glory#
319     Chapter Sixteen
320     The Gift of Failure
http://www.christiancareercenter.com/advice-and-resources/career-and-calling-articles/gift-of-failure 321 Partial rendering of Luke 8:39 King James Version (KJV) by Public Domain
322 Paraphrase of Haggai 2:9 King James Version (KJV) by Public Domain 323 Conclusion
324 Genesis 3:15 King James Version (KJV) by Public Domain 325 Ibid
326 Hebrews 8:6 King James Version (KJV) by Public Domain 327 Ibid
328     Romans 8:17 King James Version (KJV) by Public Domain
329     Paraphrase of Luke 15:12 King James Version (KJV) by Public Domain 330 Luke 15:13 King James Version (KJV) by Public Domain
331 Luke 15:15 King James Version (KJV) by Public Domain 332 Luke 15:17 King James Version (KJV) by Public Domain 333 Luke 15:18-19 King James Version (KJV) by Public Domain
334 Deuteronomy 21:17 King James Version (KJV) by Public Domain 335 12 things you need to know about the Prodigal Son
http://www.ncregister.com/blog/jimmy-akin/12-things-you-need-to-know-about-the-prodigal-son 336 Luke 15:16 King James Version (KJV) by Public Domain
337     Genesis 3:21 King James Version (KJV) by Public Domain
338     "Were Adam and Eve saved? How many children did Adam and Eve have?

When were Adam and Eve created?" http://www.gotquestions.org/Adam-and-Eve-questions.html

339    Isaiah 61:10 King James Version (KJV) by Public Domain 340 Luke 15:21 King James Version (KJV) by Public Domain

341    Paraphrase of Luke 15:18-19 King James Version (KJV) by Public Domain

342    Partial rendering of Luke 15:22 with complete rendering of Luke 23-24 King James Version (KJV) by Public Domain 343 Paraphrase of Luke 15:10 King James Version (KJV) by Public Domain

344 Luke 15:4-7 King James Version (KJV) by Public Domain 345 Luke 15:8-10 King James Version (KJV) by Public Domain 346 Luke 15:11-32 King James Version (KJV) by Public Domain 347 12 things you need to know about the Prodigal Son http://www.ncregister.com/blog/jimmy-akin/12-things-you-need-to-know-about-the-prodigal-son 348 Partial rendering of Luke 15:1 King James Version (KJV) by Public Domain

349 Partial rendering of Luke 15:2 King James Version (KJV) by Public Domain

350 Partial rendering of Luke 15:4 King James Version (KJV) by Public Domain

351 12 things you need to know about the Prodigal Son http://www.ncregister.com/blog/jimmy-akin/12-things-you-need-to-know-about-the-prodigal-son 352 Luke 15:20 King James Version (KJV) by Public Domain

353    Ibid

354    Luke 15:29 King James Version (KJV) by Public Domain 355 Luke 15:28 King James Version (KJV) by Public Domain 356 Luke 15:29 King James Version (KJV) by Public Domain

357    Paraphrase of Luke 15:31 King James Version (KJV) by Public Domain

358    Luke 15:32 King James Version (KJV) by Public Domain 359 Judges 15:16 King James Version (KJV) by Public Domain

360 Partial rendering of Judges 16:16 King James Version (KJV) by Public Domain

361 midlife crisis (noun) an emotional crisis of identity and self-confidence that can occur in early middle age. (Apple Dictionary Version 2.1.3 (80.4) Copyright © 2005–2009 Apple Inc. All rights reserved.)

362 3 Types of Change Your Brain Adapts: Reinforcing Behaviors, 1 of 3 By Athena Staik, Ph.D. http://blogs.psychcentral.com/relationships/2011/08/three-ways-your-brain-adapts-to-change-1-of-3/ 363 Partial rendering of Matthew 16:16 King James Version (KJV) by Public Domain

364    Partial rendering of Luke 22:42 King James Version (KJV) by Public Domain

365    Partial rendering of Jeremiah 2:13 King James Version (KJV) by Public

Domain 366 Analogy based on Matthew 13:22 King James Version (KJV) by Public Domain 367 2 Samuel 16:22 King James Version (KJV) by Public Domain
368     2 Samuel 12:13 King James Version (KJV) by Public Domain 369 2 Samuel 12:20 King James Version (KJV) by Public Domain

# About the Author

D r. Paul Murray is an internationally sought after speaker and preacher at leadership conferences, conventions, convocations, and global symposiums sponsored by Christian organizations, NGO's, Government entities, and at special services held by local churches. Seen on Daystar, CTN in the U.S.A, and Rede Globo in Brazil, Dr. Murray's highlights include speaking for special meetings at the United Nations in New York, NY, and Nairobi, Kenya; presenter and speaker at global leadership conferences in North and South America,

Africa and Asia; ministering and teaching at national convocations and mega-churches throughout Brazil; and as a special guest speaker for the 2014 televised, "Celebrate America" in the nation's Capital, Constitution Hall on the 4th of July.

Dr. Paul Murray is an ordained minister serving in ministry for more than twenty-five years. He is the Senior Pastor of the Lighthouse Church and holds his ministerial credentials with the Assemblies of the Lord Jesus Christ (ALJC) and with One Way Churches International (OWCI). Dr. Murray holds a leadership position within the ALJC where he is a member of the General Board. He is the District Superintendent of the New York / Mid-Atlantic Region, which oversees ministers and churches in New York, Pennsylvania, Maryland, New Jersey, Delaware and the District of Columbia.

In addition, he has established six church works under his own ministry and they are located in Maryland, Pennsylvania, New Hampshire, Georgia, and internationally in Nairobi, Kenya and Oslo, Norway. Dr. Murray's ministry and spiritual covering for his outreach efforts are blessed by his affiliation with One Way Churches International (OWCI) where he has served as their Director of World Missions.

In his passion to spiritually help others and as a result of his calling and anointing, Dr. Murray speaks at ministry conferences around the world. As an advocate for moral and innovative leadership, Dr. Murray serves as the National Co-Chairman and Executive Director of the Coalition for American Renewal, a nationwide network comprised of leaders of faith who have partnered together to re-awaken the founding values and principles that made America great.

A former Peace Corps Volunteer to the country of Tunisia, Dr. Murray has built upon his years of community service and volunteerism and infused his work ethic into his strong Christian faith to exemplify the qualities of Servant Leadership.

He holds his Doctoral Degree in Theology from Howard University's School of Divinity; a Master of Divinity in Pastoral Counseling and a Master of Art in Religion from Liberty Baptist Theological Seminary; and an undergraduate degree from the University of Phoenix where he was awarded a Bachelor of Science in Health Care Services.

Dr. Murray is a published writer, where many of his articles have been profiled in the "Apostolic Witness," an international Christian magazine. He serves on several national, regional and local non-profit boards, and has received numerous awards for his community and ministry efforts.

B.O.S.S. Publishing is a supported self-publishing services provider for minority authors looking to publish books on success, rags to riches stories, biographies, motivational, religious books, and of course, educational books.

Our mission is to create positive media for minorities. By creating positive media, we are able to illustrate to our youth and future generations that there are endless opportunities. How can our youth come to realize their potential? Public media and literature have the power to shape the self-esteem and perception of their young audiences. These messages subconsciously effects how they believe they are viewed in the world. We want to utilize this power to change the way minority youth, and audiences, in general, view the potential of African-Americans.

A major theme behind our publications is "what they see, they will believe." B.O.S.S. Publishing titles empower the reader and inspire them to become their greatest selves.

If you are interested in contributing literary works to be considered by B.O.S.S. Publishing like the one this book outlines, please contact us directly at contact@boss-publishing.com with your inquiry and submission.

Thank you for picking up this great work by an amazing author! Our hope is that it inspires you to be your own success story!

B.O.S.S. Publishing
www.boss-publishing.com

www.ingramcontent.com/pod-product-compliance
Lightning Source LLC
Chambersburg PA
CBHW060510300426
44112CB00017B/2605